MAKING HAY

Let the Wealthy and Great
Roll in Splendour and State,
I envy them not, I declare it.
I eat my own Lamb,
My Chicken and Ham,
I shear my own fleece, and I wear it.
I have lawns, I have bowers,
I have fruit, I have flowers,
The Lark is my morning alarmer.
So jolly boys now,
Here's God speed the plough
Long life and success to the Farmer!

—*The Farmer's Prayer*

To Joann
Hope you enjoy
John Jeppson

MAKING HAY

Tales from Oakholm, a Farm in Massachusetts

John Jeppson

TIDEPOOL PRESS
Cambridge, Massachusetts

Published in the United States in 2008 by TidePool Press

For information, address TidePool Press
6 Maple Avenue, Cambridge, Massachusetts 02139
www.tidepoolpress.com

Printed in China by Oceanic Graphic Printing, Inc.

Library of Congress Cataloging-in-Publication Data

Jeppson, John 1916-
    Making Hay: Tales from Oakholm, a Farm in Massachusetts
    p. cm.

ISBN 0-9755557-1-5/978-0-9755557-1-2
1. Brookfield, Massachusetts 2. Agricultural history
3. Worcester, Massachusetts 4. New England—Social History
5. Swedish-American history I. Title

This book is dedicated to my wife, Marianne

The Jeppson family and guests celebrate July Fourth at Oakholm *(1973)*

Contents

The main house at Oakholm *(1933)*

Oakholm *and its environs (1933)*
Painted by Arthur Covey

Introduction

THE YEAR, 1925 BROUGHT great sadness and great joy to the Jeppsons in Worcester. My mother's parents, John and Betty Swanstrom, died in their native Sweden, followed closely by her eldest brother, Carl. Father's mother, Thilda Jeppson, also died early that year, triggering major changes in how and where we lived. The great joy came in the form of my baby sister, Betty, who was born in April.

When Grandmother Jeppson died, the family sold the house and garden at 41 Burncoat Street and moved to her home at 1 Drury Lane, a larger house with more land in a better location. Mother and Father then decided to sell grandmother's property on Lake Quinsigamond with its two houses and lighthouse. They sold it because the area bordering Quinsigamond was being urbanized. Masses of houses were going up. Clubs were being located there—amusement parks, boat houses, stores. It was becoming noisy at night and full of people by day. The last straw was being on the wrong end of a lawsuit involving our motor boat. Against that backdrop, the second great joy in 1925 was the purchase of *Oakholm*, a farm in Brookfield, Massachusetts.

The big question before us was what should we do in summertime? Should we join the exodus to Cape Cod, or the White Mountains, or shores of Maine? Answering these questions was very easy for my father. He said, "Mother" (he addressed her as Mother whenever he wanted to make a serious pronouncement), "I refuse to become a summer bachelor who only sees his family for a day and a half on weekends and spends his evenings during the week at clubs over-eating, over-drinking and playing cards. As far as I'm concerned, our summer place has to be no more than an hour away from town. It must be on a lake and no house can be less than a quarter mile away from our own." That was that. Our father was fun to be with and, in spite of his fifty-two years, could take an active part in our outdoor games and sports. But he was also a decisive, intelligent man who expected his family to submit to his wishes. In this case, we willingly agreed. We spent several Saturday and Sunday afternoons visiting the towns and their environs that were within an hour's drive of Worcester. An hour's drive in our Franklin car on country roads—high-crowned, curved, many unpaved—meant an average speed of about twenty-five miles per hour. This effectively limited our search to an area much smaller than it would be today. Also, mother was pregnant and family hunger meant stopping for a picnic on every trip. On one occasion, an irate farmer ran us picnickers off his property. He was "damned" if he would let city-folk mess up his property or leave a gate open so his cows could get out. Mother was hard pressed to calm father down and keep him from going back to do battle with the farmer.

Our trips were unsuccessful. Places that were for sale did not meet our specifications and places that showed promise were not for sale. However, on one spring evening, Father came home to tell us that his friend and lawyer, Willis Sibley, had invited us to picnic on his farm in

Brookfield where we could see his cows and other animals. We all felt it would be a great idea and an antidote to our many unsuccessful trips. Driving the twenty-five miles took an hour and we were surprised to find no Sibleys to welcome us. We were even more surprised when Father fished a key out of his pocket and opened the door. He said Mr. Sibley had given him the key in case bad weather threatened to ruin our picnic. We were too naive, my sister Britta and I, to understand that the farm we were visiting was really for sale and that our parents were looking it over to see if they, and we, liked it.

What we found appealed immediately to all of us. Mother loved the house and view overlooking Lake Quaboag. Father imagined himself as a country squire with a horse to ride, cattle to breed and woods to manage. We children were entranced with the animals, particularly with the young ones—calves, piglets, young chickens and ducks. That evening at the supper table, our parents announced that they were buying the Sibleys' farm, and we were thrilled. In fact, we danced around the table shouting for joy. We were way too excited to eat—we didn't like the macaroni and cheese anyway. We were city folk living in Worcester, Massachusetts, and owning a farm represented a major change in our way of life.

We moved out to the farm in late June. There were oak forests all around us and the house was on a drumlin or knoll. A knoll in Swedish or Anglo-Saxon is "holm." My mother named the farm *Oakholm*.

The tales that follow are about animals, two-footed and four-footed ones, who were part of the scene at *Oakholm*. These stories begin in 1925 and end in 2007.

Lincoln Square, Worcester, Massachusetts (c. 1925)
From the collections of Worcester (MA) Historical Museum

Life In Town

LONGTIME READERS OF the *Worcester Telegram* may remember Al Banx's cartoons of the inhabitants of "Uppah" Burncoat Street. Well, I was born on lower Burncoat Street in Worcester, Massachusetts— number 41 to be exact. One hundred feet to the north of our house and across the street yawned the cavernous entrance of the Adams Square School, which I attended for two years—second and third grades. My mother taught me the equivalent of first grade at home as she felt Adams Square's first grade teacher was "less than adequate."

To the north and somewhat east was Burncoat Park with its two ponds and stone bridge where we learned to skate and where Alfred Rankin and other Scottish-Americans engaged in the ancient sport of curling. When Route 290 was built in 1974, it destroyed the school and half the park.

A little farther east was Myron Converse's farm featuring prize Guernsey cattle. Myron was the president of the Worcester Five Cents Savings Bank, later Consumers. East of him lived Kate Green, a classmate of my mother's related to one of Worcester's early families. Just a bit farther away was the Poor Farm. Behind it was located the city piggery to which all town garbage was hauled. A northeast breeze in summer brought a strong and heady aroma to our nostrils. All of this is now gone, having been usurped by the State Mutual office complex, Lincoln Plaza, the Sheraton Hotel and the Great Brook Valley apartment complex.

Directly east of our house was Green Hill Park and that has changed little. Its great hill, its ponds with their carp, its natural woods and fields, were purchased from the Green family. Also nearby was the Kelley farm at the junction of Burncoat and Lincoln streets. It was only a few acres, but there were three cows, a sow, and chickens. For us as small children it was as grand as the Bronx Zoo. We knew each beast by name and learned about the birds and the bees from the animals long before our parents reluctantly taught us the facts of life.

To the west and across Burncoat Street was the Barnard Farm, bisected by Millbrook Street. The ancient house was brick, and the large barn was painted red. We children rambled around their fields, climbed up and jumped down from their haystacks and, in general, made nuisances of ourselves. But the Barnards were tolerant of us as long as we obeyed a few rules like closing gates, not trampling hay fields, and entering barns only with permission. Route 290 eliminated the Barnard farm as well.

Immediately to the south lived the Beths, whose son Walter owned a goat. In their second story apartment resided a young couple, the Warren Davises, whose first child, Ronald, was born when I was six and already knew that the stork had not brought him. Three lots south was our favorite place, the local fire station, where neighborhood boys were always welcome—even allowed to slide down the brass pole from the second floor to the first. Fortunately, very few houses burned in our

41 Burncoat Street (1911)

neighborhood, despite coal stoves and furnaces. But with all the fields and woods around us, there were many grass and brush fires, particularly in the fall. We would often hang around the firehouse after school hoping that the alarm bell would ring. There were no sirens then, only bells, and they made a marvelous clangor.

At this time, there were no electric refrigerators. Perishable foods were kept cool by placing large blocks of ice in the top of an upright, insulated, wood structure with doors and shelves for food. It was called an icebox. Since the ice melted in a few days, it was usually delivered a couple of times every week. In fact, the ice man, in his roofed white wagon pulled by a team of powerful draft horses, drove up his assigned streets every day. He stopped at every house that had an ICE sign in a visible window. He then stepped up on a wide platform projecting a short way from the open back of the wagon, grabbed a piece of ice with a pair of steel tongs, lifted it on to a rubber cape on his back, walked to the house and swung it into the icebox. The ice men were strong. They had to be. Each block of ice weighed twenty to fifty pounds. One of my boyhood thrills was riding on the back of the ice wagon between stops sucking on a piece of ice, while the ice man drove to his next stop ringing a melodious hand-held bell to announce his coming.

Looking back on my childhood at Burncoat Street and comparing it with that of my grandchildren, I realize how lucky I was. First of all, I had great freedom. Because there were so few automobiles, our parents let us cross streets and roam for miles. Although Worcester had a larger population than it does now, there was much more undeveloped land. There was less urban sprawl. We could live in the country, yet walk "down street" to shop at the Worcester Market across from the Salisbury Mansion. We walked to Mechanics Hall to hear Music Festival concerts, and to our church on Belmont Street on Sundays. Lincoln Square was a marvel to me as a little boy. It was the hub of a giant wheel, the spokes being Main, Highland, Grove, Lincoln, Belmont, Summer, and Union streets. There were trolley lines on five of these streets. Two parallel Boston & Maine Railroad tracks bisected the "wheel." One traffic cop regulated cars, trolleys and horse-pulled wagons that were coming at him from every point on the compass. He was amazing. My parents told me he had eyes at the back of his head, which puzzled me because I could never see them. My father gave him a box of cigars at Christmas, driving his car up to the officer's high platform, with its enclosed railing and umbrella, to hand him the gift. All the traffic stopped as this small annual ceremony took place.

Even though we lived amid bucolic surroundings on Burncoat Street, we spent at least part of our summers on the shores of Lake Quinsigamond, on the Shrewsbury side, at my grandparents' place, *King's Point.* It was a magic spot for me, with a cobblestone lighthouse at the end of the point, an octagonal tea house on a knoll where cookies and cambric tea were dispensed to children at appointed times. A stream meandered down the slope through a rock garden with several miniature waterfalls. There was a large inboard motorboat with a spoked steering wheel that my grandfather captained while my grandmother sat stiffly and apprehensively in the stern in a wicker chair. We particularly enjoyed the automatic sprinkling system on the lawns, running through sprays on hot days.

It is clear to me now that our parents and grandparents did not live extravagantly, but life was gracious. There were local delivery services. Milk and eggs were left at our doorstep in the morning. Groceries were delivered from a phoned-in order. Railway Express picked up our trunks and bags and delivered them to the far-off places we visited by boat or train. There were several kinds of other door-to-door services: laundry, telegraph, knife sharpening, and fruit delivery. Our parents and grandparents in many ways lived a far more comfortable life than we do now.

THE JEPPSON FAMILY lived at 1 Drury Lane in Worcester from 1918 to 1942 when my father, George Nathaniel Jeppson and his wife, Selma Ulrika Swanstrom, donated the property to Worcester Polytechnic Institute. Designed by architect Lucius Briggs, the house was built shortly after the turn of the century by a man named Woodland who

The port cochère at 1 Drury Lane (1920)

had changed his name from Skøgland when he arrived from Sweden. We know little about him, except the rumor that he had committed suicide after severe financial losses. As children, we convinced ourselves that this terrible event had taken place in the front hall lavatory where we were certain the cracks in the white tile had been caused by the fatal bullet. We were a hard-hearted lot. We never hesitated to take impressionable young friends to see the lavatory. They were sworn to secrecy. Much later I learned that Mr. Woodland poisoned himself due to failing health and not financial losses.

My grandfather, John Jeppson, and his wife, Thilda Ahlstrom, were the first Jeppsons to own 1 Drury Lane. In 1918 they moved from a home near Norton Company on West Boylston Street at Barber's Crossing. John had chosen to build that house in order to be close to the factory he had planned and managed. He was seventy-five and Thilda was seventy-three when 1 Drury Lane was purchased.

Although I was only four when my grandfather died in 1920, I remember his tall, patriarchal figure and his full white beard. However, I was too young to witness an evening ritual that made clear just who was really in charge of the Jeppson household. Every evening, Grandfather relaxed with whiskey and soda and a cigar. After dinner, he would sit in a leather chair near the living room fireplace and blow smoke up the chimney. When he finished his cigar, he would walk quietly to the front door, open it and discreetly throw the ashes and the cigar butt under the rhododendrons. Although he was the production boss at Norton Company, he was definitely Number Two in his own house.

Thilda Ahlstrom Jeppson (1918)
Portraits by Emily Burling Waite

John Jeppson (1918)

Grandmother lived at 1 Drury Lane until her death in 1925. My elder sister, Britta Dorothy, and I spent most winter weekends with her. We arrived in time for tea on Saturday afternoon and left for Sunday school the next morning. Grandmother served wonderful Sunday breakfasts—fruit juice, rectangular strips of cornmeal mush, bacon and apple rings awash in maple syrup. We always read the funnies—*The Katzenjammer Kids, Mutt and Jeff, Barney Google* and a miniature magazine cut out of *The Boston Globe* called *The Little Delineator*. Breakfast was served in an upstairs sitting room at the north end of the corridor.

Grandmother was a strong character, very much the matriarch. She dressed only in black after her husband's death. She had a full figure, tightly corseted, and she walked with two canes, arthritis having taken its toll. She was also quite hard of hearing at a time when electric hearing aids were rare and cumbersome. She compensated by cleverly using a three-foot rubber hose covered in black silk. One end was held up to her ear, and the other to the mouth of whoever was trying to speak to her. She, and we, became adept at this method of communication.

Grandmother often held court in what we called the North Porch. French doors opened to the east terrace and green tile floors. She always sat in a wicker fan chair surrounded by palms and other large plants— every inch the queen. One of her favorite occupations was supervising great meals in the dining room. Her Thanksgivings, Christmases, and birthday celebrations were especially memorable as was the dining room, with ceiling and walls delicately plastered in the style of Robert Adam who had so much influence on Georgian art and architecture in the eighteenth century. My wife, Marianne, and I now have the dining room furniture formerly in that room.

Adjacent to the dining room, the butler's pantry led into the kitchen which had a maid's sitting room and a kitchen pantry next to it. These four rooms were our favorite haunts as children. This being before refrigerators, the kitchen pantry contained a large icebox that needed to be filled regularly with blocks of ice. In order to eliminate the need for the iceman to enter the kitchen, the icebox opened at the back so that ice could be loaded from the kitchen entryway in the pantry. There was a large flour barrel under one of the counters that could be swung out when bread and cakes were being made. Other counters and cupboards contained various crocks filled with eggs, pickles and cookies as well as boxes of spices and herbs. The aromas from the kitchen area were always enticing.

My grandmother, Thilda, died during the Christmas season in 1925. I remember her funeral well. She lay in state in the living room, as my grandfather had five years earlier. Six months after she died, my father and mother moved into 1 Drury Lane with their three children: Britta, me, and new baby, Betty Thilda. My father at that time was works manager of the Norton Company, the largest manufacturer of abrasives in the world, and was in charge of all production.

For us, the new house was a marvel. It had an in-house telephone system connecting all of the bedrooms. A system of bells rang individually in the kitchen indicating when and where service was needed. There was a series of racks in the cellar that rolled wet clothes into a gas drier to dry them after washing. There was a "mangle" to wring water out of sheets and tablecloths. The floors on the north and south porches were heated with embedded steam pipes—an early version of radiant heating. The most unusual modern convenience at 1 Drury Lane was a central vacuum cleaning system with a hose outlet in every room. Also wondrous to us were the five bathrooms on the second floor. There was even a laundry chute connecting the first and second floors with the basement. My bedroom was over the front porch. Its west window opened onto the roof over the *porte cochère*, providing me a way to shimmy down a column to the ground. Telltale finger marks on the column usually gave me away.

Even the three-car garage had a contraption that was new to us, an overhead, large-diameter wheel attached to a hose used for washing the car beneath it. This eliminated the need for dragging the hose over or around the car. The garage also had a chauffeur's room. It was presided over in my grandmother's time by a man named Larson. He was tall, blond and mustachioed, and wore a black uniform complete with *puttees*. The garage housed two Pierce Arrows. One was an open touring car with a large trunk in the rear, spare tires to the side and a fitted picnic basket. The other was a later model with a fully enclosed passenger area. Grandmother took us on summer trips to Boston, Revere, and Plymouth. Those trips are among my favorite childhood memories, but I seem to recall the sumptuous picnics more than the interesting places we saw. I can still see my grandmother, with veils securing her hat against the wind, sitting next to her visored and dignified chauffeur.

My father and mother did very little to change the structure of the house. Another entrance was added for servants and children. This allowed us to hang coats and store dirty boots without disturbing the pristine sanctity of the front hall or kitchen. A billiard room was added in the basement. The room had two doors, each with a small stained glass window decorated with Viking ships designed by my father.

My mother, Selma, was a horticulturist who had an instinctive sense of good garden design. At our previous home on Burncoat Street, she had created a lovely garden. The little formal garden at the south end of Drury Lane was not enough for her, so she laid out the terrace to the east, adding walls and stone pillars. It had a few shrubs outside its walls and a beautiful perennial garden inside. It was often used for garden parties. The square tops of the stone pillars provided an ideal vantage point for watching baseball games at nearby Worcester Polytechnic Institute.

The walled backyard was a favorite hangout for us children. There were long clotheslines on the east side. In the center was a large Norway maple, our favorite climbing tree. It also provided shade for a massive doghouse with two rooms and a hinged shingle roof. This had been built originally for Grandmother's dog, Ned, a large German shepherd, who, fortunately, was gentle with children.

Although my mother and father were both born in Worcester, their parents were from Sweden and this Scandinavian heritage influenced our lives deeply. We learned Swedish as children, attended a Swedish Lutheran Church, observed Swedish customs, and ate Swedish foods on holidays. We also traveled abroad to visit our many Swedish relations—aunts, uncles, and cousins in the "old country." Swedish art was featured at 1 Drury Lane. Two paintings by the Swedish impressionist Anders Zorn graced our living room. They are both now in the Worcester Art Museum. Bird and animal paintings by Bruno Liljefors were in several rooms, as were etchings by Zorn and Carl Larson.

Distinguished Swedes, businessmen, bankers, and diplomats, were regularly entertained at 1 Drury Lane. Our most renowned visitors

The terrace gardens at 1 Drury Lane (1929)

were the Crown Prince of Sweden, Gustav Adolph, and his wife, Lady Louise Mountbatten. He became King Gustav VI. She was the sister of Louis Mountbatten, a hero in World War II and the last British Viceroy of India. The Crown Prince and his wife visited Worcester in June of 1926. A lunch was held for them on our east terrace under an awning specially made for the occasion. They spent several hours at the house and were quite friendly to my two sisters and me.

Gunnar Myrdal, winner of the Nobel Prize for economics in 1974, and his wife, Swedish ambassador to India, also visited 1 Drury Lane. His work on race relations in the U.S., *American Dilemma: the Negro Problem and Modern Democracy*, became a seminal book on the topic.

Eminent Americans also graced our table. Calvin Coolidge visited while he was governor of Massachusetts. Father later visited him at the White House. Joe Martin, long time Congressman from Massachusetts and later Speaker of the House, was another luncheon guest. These were private occasions. Father was a Republican stalwart in Central Massachusetts, which was overwhelmingly Democratic. *Oakholm* was a wonderful counterpoint to the formal lives we led in Worcester.

John Jeppson's sister, Britta, dressed in Swedish costume, under the awning created for the visit of the Crown Prince of Sweden to 1 Drury Lane (1926)

Part One

A Country Squire

George Nathaniel Jeppson and his horse (1925)

A Country Squire

My FATHER, George Nathaniel Jeppson, was a man of parts. His immigrant Swedish parents sent him to what they considered the best high school in Worcester, the Highland Military Academy. They financed his training as an engineer at the Royal School of Mines in Sweden. But they didn't spoil their only child. He was required to care for the horse, clean the kerosene lamps, weed the garden, shovel the snow, and help his father maintain the house and barn. Sunday school in the Lutheran church was never missed and lessons had to be learned before bedtime. In spite of all these duties, he had time to play baseball, sail on Indian Lake, and dance polkas and waltzes at well-chaperoned balls.

During his school years he learned to play cornet and piano so well that he almost took up a musical career. He played until the week before he died at the age of eighty-nine. The family was regularly treated to his accomplished renditions of Beethoven sonatas in the evenings. However, it was business that claimed the majority of his time and interest. At age twenty-four, he was employed at the Norton Company, a small abrasives manufacturing company founded in 1885 and managed by his father John Jeppson I, Milton P. Higgins, and a group of local investors. He eventually became president and CEO and played a major role in developing Norton into a world-wide leader in the abrasives manufacturing and machine tool industries with over twelve thousand employees. Well into his seventies he was still developing processes for the manufacture of Norton's product lines, including patenting a new method of manufacturing ceramic grinding wheels.

Apart from his business life, he supported causes—political and non-profit—in his beloved city of Worcester, Massachusetts. He was instrumental in organizing the merger of three Lutheran churches into the Trinity Lutheran Church. He chaired the building committee which followed every detail of the design and construction process until the last brick was placed in what he called Worcester's Lutheran cathedral. The extensive panels adorning the ceiling of the knave were painted by his friend Arthur Covey whose murals of *Oakholm* are on the cover of this book.

My father's busy city life did not deter him from spending as much time in the country as he could, hiking with the Appalachian Mountain Club or taking his family on drives to see beautiful rural places. He often reminisced of his childhood when his parents and he lived in the small village of West Sterling, Massachusetts and he walked two and a half miles to a one-room school house. Our bedtime stories consisted of tales of farming with "Farmer Hank" as the main character and a disreputable villain named Hiram who stole eggs from under chickens.

In 1925, at the age of fifty-two, Father was at last in a position to buy a country place. He was then Works Manager of the Norton Company in charge of all production operations. My mother was caring for three children and expanding her interests in horticulture and landscape design. He had the wherewithal to buy a property, a skilled wife to help manage and develop it, and a fast car to get him to work on time in the morning. Life was good. The business and family were thriving. He was about to acquire the missing piece, a farm in the country.

The Norton Company plant in Worcester, Massachusetts (1978)

Daisy

MY PARENTS, SISTERS, and I moved into *Oakholm* on a Friday in June in 1925. The next day at breakfast, my father said to me, "John, I want to show you something in the red barn." I told him that I had already been and knew what was there—Molly and Bess, the two Percheron workhorses, and a big sow with eight piglets. But Father said, "Well, come with me anyway. I think there is something you missed." So, I dutifully followed him into the barn. There, in the one and only box stall, was a beautiful Shetland pony.

Her name was Daisy. She was a bay mare with a white star on her forehead, black markings below her front knees and low white socks above the rear hooves. Her tail and mane were jet black and she was a petite four feet high at the withers—the ridge between her shoulder blades. To me, she was the most beautiful animal that God had ever created. My walking into the stall didn't disturb her a bit. Nor was she bothered when I ran my hands over her head and back down her legs. When she looked at me with her great limpid eyes, it was love at first sight. Daisy was eight years old, as was I, and seemed to have an especially good disposition. She was perfect in every way.

But was I ever wrong. The honeymoon lasted only two days, the two days it took to find her a saddle and bridle. During that time, I proudly led her around with a rope clipped to a halter on her head. First, I took her to the house to show her off to my mother and sisters, and then down the road to the neighbors, and finally to the lake for a drink of water. She behaved well during this time. In fact, I was worried that she might be too docile.

Saddle and bridle arrived on the third morning. I walked confidently into Daisy's stall with a shining new saddle in my hands and placed it on the pony. No reaction. Then, I reached under Daisy to grab the girth. As I tried to pull up the girth strap to the buckle, Daisy inhaled an enormous quantity of air. This swelled her belly so much that I could not pull the strap to the buckle. The farmer's son, Reuben, an eighteen-year-old who was watching my feeble efforts, said, "Let me give you a hand."

At first, he was unsuccessful as well, until he realized that she had to exhale periodically. When she let the air out of her lungs, he quickly fastened the girth. Putting on the bridle presented another challenge. Daisy clenched her teeth when I tried to put the bit in her mouth. Reuben came to my rescue again by pressing a thumb behind her teeth which forced her to open her mouth allowing me to insert the bit. She was now saddled and bridled.

Still optimistic, I led her outside the barn ready to mount. I gathered up the reins, placed my foot in the stirrup and swung my other leg over her to seat myself in the saddle. Daisy took a swift sidestep to the right that sent me tumbling ignominiously to the ground. By this time my eight-year old ego hit bottom. I was ready to quit horseback riding forever, even though I had yet to sit on a horse—let alone ride one.

John Jeppson, age eight, successfully riding Daisy (1925)

Daisy

Reuben helped me up. His father, Farmer Brown, got into the act as well. He assured me that all would be well. "All you have to do is show the pony who's boss," he said. He gave me a freshly cut switch from a nearby maple tree, which I was supposed to use if Daisy misbehaved again. He held her while I gathered the reins and got in the saddle—this time without mishap. Then I tapped her lightly with my heels and "clucked" the go-ahead sound. Nothing happened. She didn't move. Farmer Brown said, "Switch her, and let her know who's boss." So I did. Daisy jumped forward, and reared and bucked. I hung on for dear life, but she still refused to walk forward. Now all three of us were annoyed. Brown and Reuben, both with switches, got her going at last, but when they turned to walk home, she made a beeline toward the barn. That was my first ride.

Eventually, I got her going on a regular basis, but each ride was eventful. Trotting down the road, she kept her eyes peeled for low-lying branches hoping they would knock me off or scrape my leg or knee. The happiest day of my young life was when my family realized that I had grown too big for Daisy. She was sold to friends who evidently knew the ways of Shetland ponies better than we did. We never heard them say nasty things about her.

However, I was not yet fully liberated from Daisy. Several years later, when I was in sixth grade at Bancroft School in Worcester, I was tapped to be one of the Three Kings in the Christmas pageant. On the stage were Mary and Joseph, played by high school students, and the baby Jesus, played by a real baby, the son of one of the school parents. Joining them were several live animals to give the scene the genuine feel of a stable. As one of the Three Kings, bearing incense as a gift for

35

the baby Jesus, I climbed up the staircase to the stage. I almost lost my crown, and the incense to boot, when I saw Daisy looking balefully at me from her position next to the manger.

Hiawatha

THE MAIN HOUSE at *Oakholm* was modest—a typical Cape Cod home inside and out. It was shingled with white trim and green blinds. The front door led into a hall with a straight staircase directly ahead, a dining room to the left, and a living room to the right. The kitchen and pantry were directly behind the dining room. Upstairs were four bedrooms and a bathroom. It was a simple home, but light and airy inside. The surrounding fields, lakes, and woods gave it a magical feeling.

Betty, my youngest sister, was born the year we bought the house. I was seven. Since Mother was quite ill at that time, a nurse, Miss Bishop, arrived to take care of Mother and her new child. Bish, as we called her, had great stories to tell of her childhood in Newfoundland and her nursing career with the famous Sir Wilfred Grenfell at his mission in Labrador. She told stories of people rescued off the ice and snow and taken by dog sleds to Grenfell's clinic. Bish became an integral part of our lives.

My mother and father loved *Oakholm* so much that they wanted to share it with others. This often took the form of parties. In order to make these affairs memorable, my parents always planned something special, usually with a theme of some sort. One party I'll never forget

The main house at Oakholm *before later additions (1927)*

was given to honor one of my father's business associates at Norton Company, Pierre Baruzy. A French national and a truly colorful character, Pierre was not only a good business executive, but he was also the amateur middleweight boxing champion of Europe, and a superb gymnast and diver.

The time for the party arrived on a beautiful June day with a light westerly breeze that was just strong enough to provide comfort and help blow mosquitoes away. The hay fields had not yet been cut. The timothy, clover, and other grasses undulated like a green sea as the breeze flowed over them. The gardens around the house were in a state of perfection and the few light clouds in the sky were mirrored in the deep blue of the lake. All was right with the world.

At six o'clock the guests began to arrive, about twenty in all, and were served cold drinks on the lawn. After everyone had come, Father announced that he, Mother, and the guest of honor, Baruzy, would lead them on a short walk through the woods and down the hill on the north side of the house. The guests would see some of the natural beauty of *Oakholm* and work up their appetites for the lobster feast to follow.

At the bottom of the hill, they came to an opening in the woods with a clear view of a grass-covered hill to their left. Suddenly, they were astonished to see five Quaboag Indian braves on horseback on the crest, each in stark silhouette against the setting sun. Uttering loud high-pitched cries, the "Indians" galloped down the hill toward the "palefaces" whom they quickly surrounded. The Quaboags singled out Baruzy, tied his hands and looped a rope around his neck. They dragged him into the woods and disappeared as quickly as they came.

My father and mother calmed the anxious guests, by letting them know that the Quaboags were usually a friendly tribe. Why had the warriors singled out Baruzy? Father speculated that Baruzy's red hair might have inflamed them. He explained that Indians had hated red hair ever since the ferocious and red-haired Leif Eriksson and his Vikings had invaded their shores. Father also assured the guests that there was safety in numbers. If they would care to join Mother and him, they would form a search party and attempt a rescue.

Following a path into the woods, they soon came upon a majestic grove of white pines, some over one hundred feet high, casting a deep shade on the heavy carpet of needles beneath them. This was what my mother called her "cathedral." She often came there for rest and reflection. But this day an amazing sight met the nervous guests. A large bonfire lit up the center of the grove. On the far side of it, tied to a large strong stake, was Pierre, disheveled and terrified. As the group entered the grove, fifteen braves and squaws began to dance around the fire and Baruzy, stomping their feet, making bloodcurdling cries, and brandishing spears and tomahawks. The braves on horseback were poised nearby ready to take orders from the chief, a tall Indian wearing a feathered headdress.

Undaunted, Father approached the chief with his right hand raised to shoulder height, palm outward to show his peaceful intentions. Peace pipes appeared and were smoked by the principals. There was much talk and more dancing. At last, a now-laughing Baruzy was untied and allowed to rejoin the guests. Mother and Father introduced the Indians to the crowd. They were members of the Louise Galaway Players, a summer stock company whose theater was Brookfield's town hall. Louise Galaway, a former Broadway luminary, played the leading squaw. She was ably abetted by Rose Dresser, head of the drama department at the Winsor School, and Zazu Pitts, one of Hollywood's great character actors and comedians. The braves on horseback included Swen Pulson, a cousin, and two young neighbors, Loring Coes and his brother, Rufus Putnam Coes. Rufus was insufferably proud to be named after his ancestor General Putnam, the founder of Marietta, Ohio. I led the group on a Welsh pony called "Nip."

The tableau was supposed to end after drinks and hors d'oeuvres served by squaws who emerged from a large teepee. However, a delightful unplanned act followed. Rising to the occasion, one of the guests, Clifford Anderson, called for attention and in a mellifluous baritone recited the conclusion to Longfellow's poem, *Hiawatha*.

Thus departed Hiawatha,
Hiawatha the Beloved,
In the glory of the sunset,
In the purple mists of evening,
To the regions of the home-wind
Of the Northwest-Wind, Keewaydin,
To the Islands of the Blessed,
To the Kingdom of Ponemah
To the Land of the Hereafter!

Galloping through the fields (1927)

Flies and Bacilli

A FARMER AND his family came with our purchase of *Oakholm.* They lived in an old yellow house across the road from the main house which we called the farmhouse. Farmer Brown and Father had no use for each other from the very beginning. Brown, a tough Vermonter, brooked no interference when it came to farming, including care of animals, barns, fields and equipment. In Brown's eyes, Father was a city slicker and an absolute greenhorn. Father, on the other hand, felt that Brown was too lazy and ran a disorderly agricultural operation.

The last straw occurred when Father told Brown that he wanted to eliminate flies from the cow barn. "Flies!" said Brown, "Any damn fool knows you can't have a barn without flies. They come in with the cows at milking." Undaunted, Father bought a gross of flypaper, the kind you hang from above and pull down into a two-inch wide spiral strip about two feet long. With a small boy's help—me—he hung sixty of them in the cow barn. We put them in the space between two parallel mangers where the cows faced each other, locked in their stanchions for milking and feeding. After a week, we counted the flies caught on six of the strips, averaged them out at a figure of 533 per strip, and multiplied by sixty to get a pretty accurate total of 31,980. Quite a haul.

It took Father very little time to come up with a simple way to keep the flies out of the barn altogether. He put up screens on all the windows and doors. Two of the windows were fitted with electric screens. He then bought a hand spray gun, the type with a push-and-pull handle, to be used by someone standing at the door when the cows came in. That person sprayed each cow and closed the door after the last cow entered. *Flit* was a popular bug spray at that time. One of their most successful ad campaigns, showing a giant mosquito chasing a woman shouting, "Quick, Henry! The Flit", was originated by Theodore Geisel who later achieved fame and fortune as Dr. Seuss.

As a result of this concentrated effort, the fly population at *Oakholm* dropped sharply and at one point I heard Mother turn to Father and use that old expression, "There are no flies on you, George!" We surmised that the lack of flies was also appreciated by the cows who produced more milk because they did not have to swish their tails around so much.

Something else happened during that first year that was even more momentous than the elimination of flies—a tragic event with a positive outcome. Mother learned that cows could carry the tuberculosis bacillus without showing any of the outward signs of the disease. Milk from an infected cow could transmit the disease to humans. At that time, there were no regulations requiring that dairy cows be tested for tuberculosis. Tuberculosis was then a worldwide scourge affecting millions of people, and there was no known cure for it. Sulfa drugs and penicillin, which eventually eradicated the disease, would not be readily available for another twenty years. When Mother brought up the question of testing our herd of Guernseys, we laughed. Father said, "Look how healthy all our animals are. They couldn't look any better." We children nodded our approval and told mother not to worry. But worry she did. She kept after Father until he called the veterinarian and arranged to have our entire herd—cows, heifers, and calves—tested. Every animal proved positive for tuberculosis, and within a few days every animal was trucked away to the slaughterhouse. Interiors of the barns and sheds were painted and disinfected. Barnyards and pastures lay fallow for a full year. This allowed rain, sun, and freezing temperatures to kill the bacilli in the soil. Sad as we were at the loss of our herd, we felt proud of Mother who saved us and our customers from the feared disease.

Oakholm was now without flies and without cows. It was also without Farmer Brown who was fed up with the crazy Jeppsons and their high falutin' ideas.

Quick, Henry! the Flit *from Theodore Geisel's ad campaign (c.1928)*

King

WITH THE DEPARTURE of Farmer Brown and his family, and the slaughter of the infected cattle, one might expect that Father's ambitions as a country squire would have been discouraged. Not at all. He swiftly shifted his attention to another project—the acquisition of two horses—one for himself and one for my older sister, Britta. A five-gaited, deep-chested black gelding belonging to a doctor in Southbridge was for sale, and seemed to be exactly the right animal for Father. In his new riding britches, puttees, and high shoes, he had a trial ride on the horse. "King," as he was named, was gentle and "neck-wise." This meant that a touch of the reins on either side of his neck would signal him to turn, and there was no need to pull the reins attached to the bit in the horse's mouth. King was beautifully gaited and smooth to ride. And the price was right. Father bought him on the spot, and brought him to *Oakholm* the next day where he was led into a box stall for all of us to see. On the following Saturday morning, we gathered at the barn to see Squire Jeppson take his first ride around his domain on his beautiful new horse. The sun was shining.

Father led King out of his stall and clipped ropes on either side of his halter. The ropes were attached to hooks on each side of the barn's

GNJ on King (1927)

carriage room to hold him while he was being saddled and bridled. The moment that King felt he was tied up, he went berserk. He reared up and hit the ceiling before falling on his back. He kicked and thrashed his newly shod hooves in every direction. Father barely escaped with his life. This episode would have daunted anyone else, but not Father. King eventually calmed down, having freed himself from his halter—still shaking and sweating from the ordeal. He stood quietly while Father fed him a few lumps of sugar and led him back to his stall. Father rightly deduced that King could not stand being tied in any way. For the many years he was ridden, King was never tied. He was watered, fed, saddled, bridled, groomed, and clipped without being attached to anything. He and Father became fast friends. King would nicker when Father came to the stall and nuzzle him until he got his daily lump of sugar. He stood quietly while being mounted and knew exactly where Father wanted to go and what gait to use: walk, single foot, trot, canter, or gallop. He seemed to know when his rider wished to stop to look at a view, and when he was allowed to put his head down for a drink from a running brook. They were a well-matched pair and good friends. Father could never fathom how he had bought this handsome horse so reasonably until he learned that King had killed his previous owner, the Southbridge doctor, who made the fatal mistake of trying to tie him down.

Stellan Peterson

FATHER DIDN'T HAVE to look very long or far for a replacement for Farmer Brown. He had met Stellan Peterson, a young Swede, several times. Stellan was then engaged to Hildur, our cook. Father had had several communications with him while he was waiting for his fiancée to appear. He had learned that Stellan had been brought up in Sweden in a province known for its beauty and good farms and he had worked as a forester, carpenter, and farmer. Arriving in the United States in 1923, he soon landed a job as a carpenter at the Norton Company in Worcester, where Father was then Works Manager. They liked and respected each other almost immediately, and Stellan quickly accepted the offer to become the boss farmer at *Oakholm* complete with a house to live in. Having a new home enabled Hildur and Stellan to be married. The ceremony took place at our house at 1 Drury Lane. I can see them now, a handsome athletic couple, doing an energetic *schottische* together and dancing round the maypole at Mother's birthday parties. They lived and worked at *Oakholm* for more than fifty years.

When Stellan and Hildur arrived at *Oakholm* in 1925, it was not the same as it is now. It was much smaller in terms of land and buildings. Farming was different, too. It was very much as it had been in the days

Stellan and Hildur Peterson with daughter, Evelyn (1930)

of our early pioneers. Cows were milked by hand; rocks were moved with a crowbar; and hay was handled with a pitchfork. Horses were the only help to manpower. Stellan was strong and he was smart. He and Father kept up with the most modern agricultural methods. They designed and constucted buildings, reclaimed land, improved forests, and developed fine herds of cattle. It was a sad day for his family and for ours when cancer killed Stellan at the age of eighty-three in 1978. A charitable trust was established to honor him.

The Three Graces

In 1925, we were a household of eight: my father and mother, two sisters and me, and we gained three others who were not blood relatives. Anna Skoog (*skoog* translates from the Swedish to "forest") was our cook. Hulda Hanson was in charge of the upstairs, waited on table and looked after our domestic bestiary of dogs, cats, and a canary. Anna Nygren (*nygren* translates from Swedish to "new green") was general *factotum* and housekeeper who pitched in wherever necessary. They were born in Sweden, but all had become American citizens. We dubbed them the "Three Graces."

Skoogie and Hulda had wonderful singsong Swedish accents. "Th" became "T" and "J" became "Y". For example, Hulda would say to me, "Yon, pick up your 'tings', or I'll tell your mutter." Anna Skoog called Mother "Mrs. Yeppson" and made delicious raspberry "yam." On the other hand, Anna Nygren spoke the King's English and even corrected me when I made grammatical mistakes. One blonde, the other grey-haired, the two Annas were tall and sturdy. Hulda was shorter and brunette. When visiting friends or relatives on days off, they dressed "to the nines" and wore elegant hats. One day, Mother bought a handsome fitted coat with a fur collar at her favorite shop on Newbury Street in

Boston. She was chagrined to find that Anna Nygren—when dressed for her next day off—was wearing the exact same coat. Anna had bought it at Richard Healy's in Worcester for half the price.

The farmhouse at *Oakholm* was their first residence in Brookfield. It had been enlarged to include a three-bedroom apartment with a living room and fireplace for Hulda and the two Annas. The house also had an apartment and an office for Stellan Peterson and his family. However, this arrangement never really worked. Stellan and his bride had two daughters in rapid succession and soon needed more room. Disputes and altercations developed to the point where my parents designed and built an attractive wing on their house for their three "ladies." They enlarged the kitchen and added a bathroom and a nursery for my newborn sister, Betty. This was the first of three additions to the house.

During the summer, the Annas and Hulda often had an afternoon swim in the lake. They dressed in bathing suits with skirts, pants, stockings and shower caps. As a young boy, I could only guess about the good figures lurking beneath all that black material. When I was a bit older, I would take them for rowboat rides on lakes Quaboag and Quacumquasit. If the weather was bad, we arranged to have them driven to the Casino Theater in Ware to see films starring the likes of Charlie Chaplin, Douglas Fairbanks and Mary Pickford.

We made ice cream in a wooden bucket with a crank and dry ice. I enjoyed manning the crank, which entitled me to the first taste of ice cream. We canned large quantities of home-grown apples, peaches, plums, tomatoes and beans outside on a two-burner kerosene stove, which kept the kitchen from getting overheated on hot summer days. Pickling was done in large earthenware jugs in the cool of the cellar.

From left, *Hulda Hanson, Anna Nygren and Anna Skoog*
with Betty (1926)

    This wonderful threesome decided to retire at about the same time in their middle seventies, just after World War II and after forty years living with our family. Mother was faced with the challenge of finding their replacements. Ingeborg soon arrived on our doorstep. Fresh from Sweden and highly recommended, she was a nice looking, dark-haired, slightly heavy woman of forty-five. She immediately took over the kitchen. Her first meals were outstanding. Among other things, she produced a *smörgåsbord* for a party my wife, Marianne, and I gave.

It was marvelous, except that Yankee Doodle, our Dalmatian, cleverly filched small amounts from each dish without disturbing the plate as a whole—something we did not discover until our guests arrived.

Unfortunately, Ingeborg had a major handicap that made her stay at *Oakholm* very brief. She hated hot weather. Having come from a town in northern Sweden where the weather in summer was always cool, she found our "dog days" of summer unbearable. On the first warm days she experienced in Brookfield, she took off all the screens in the kitchen and in her apartment in order to get more fresh air. This let in an inconsequential amount of additional air, and a hoard of mosquitoes. Naturally, my parents were displeased. The screens were quickly re-installed and new electric fans pacified Ingeborg in the short term.

But the end came when my father visited the kitchen early one summer morning ready for breakfast. Standing there stark naked was Ingeborg. She shrieked and father beat a hasty retreat. It seemed she had never worked for a master of the house who entered the kitchen at breakfast time, and in order to keep cool, she had stripped off all her clothes. Ingeborg left soon thereafter. We later heard that she had found a satisfactory position in an air-conditioned house in Philadelphia.

Prince

AN INN SINCE 1771, the Publick House in Sturbridge, Massachusetts, is primarily known nowadays for its fine restaurant. The restaurant's main room is the former barn, a building I knew as a home for horses and cows, but especially horses. A fellow named Snodgrass rented half the barn for his livery stable where he bought and sold horses.

My father, my older sister Britta, and I stopped there on a grey, August day in 1926 to see if Snodgrass had a horse suitable for Britta. He brought out several animals for us to look over—a stocky Morgan with an army brand, a western Pinto pony, and a tall, American standard with a black mane and white blaze, to whom Britta took an instant liking. She was allowed to saddle and bridle him and ride around Sturbridge Town Common. His manners were good. He was steady and smooth gaited. Although Father thought the horse was too big for my sister, she prevailed by threatening to leave home if she couldn't have Prince, for that was his name. Prince was harness trained, so he could pull carriages and do light farm work. Snodgrass hitched him to a Concord buggy to show how well he performed when pulling.

Father bought Prince, the Concord buggy, the harness, and the aforementioned army-trained Morgan. The purchase of the Morgan

From left, *Britta on Prince, John on Tuck and GNJ on King
in front of the hay barn (1928)*

surprised Britta and me, but Father said, "We will have friends visiting us from time to time, and we will need a dependable extra horse for them to ride." Ginger was indeed a good, solid animal with no bad habits, but he was rough gaited. For a dozen years, he was the "extra" horse at *Oakholm*.

Sturbridge was only six miles from *Oakholm*, so Father rode Ginger back to our barn. Britta and I drove Prince in the Concord buggy, and Snodgrass drove our car, followed by a hired man in his car to provide a means for his return. Mother was aghast to see this little parade drive up to the farm. She said, "George, where in the world are you going to put two more horses and a buggy? You already have King and Daisy, and Molly and Bess! There's no room for more!"

Father replied, "There will be room when I build a new horse barn!"

And that's what he did. It was the first of several new buildings at *Oakholm* designed by my father. It still stands today just south of the cow barn, a testimony to Father's architectural ability.

Britta continued to ride and drive Prince for many years. She particularly enjoyed hitching him up to the buggy and driving the two-and-a-half miles to Brookfield to do errands for her mother, such as picking up groceries at Ken's market, buying magazines, needles and thread for sewing and a candy bar for herself at Frazier's News.

Betty, our younger sister, thirteen years younger than Britta, joined her on one of these journeys. Betty was then seven, Britta twenty. The day was perfect. The time was mid-morning. Prince trotted along pleasantly, slowing to walk up the hills. The route took them past pastures with cows placidly chewing their cuds, past Coe's farm and its fine view of Lake Quaboag, across the causeway under its giant willows surrounded by marshes, over the railroad bridge with the old five-story gummed paper mill on the right, up the hill to the Brookfield town common, finally taking a right turn onto Central Street. Her destination lay just past the fire house and town hall. Prince wasn't even breathing hard, and young Betty was bored with the slow-paced half-hour drive and lack of excitement along the way. They made their purchases: a magazine, the *Saturday Evening Post*, four cans of peaches, two candy bars, two root beers, and two boxes of Gorton's dried cod fish.

The Oakholm *barns (c. 1930)*

They started back and got as far as the watering trough just before reaching the railroad bridge. All was well. Prince enjoyed the fresh cool water. Betty and Britta each had a bite of their chocolate bars and a swig of root beer. Then an ominous sound was heard in the distance. Britta knew what it was. She tightened the reins, gave Prince a gentle tap with the buggy whip, and headed for the railroad bridge hoping to get over it before the train arrived. She didn't. The steam locomotive pulling a long freight train hit the bridge at the same moment that she, Prince, the buggy and Betty did—the train under it, Britta and company over it. The steam from the locomotive engulfed them. The noise was awesome. Prince reared up on his hind legs, let out a scream, and took off. His racing genes took over and he ran full speed ahead for two miles with Britta "sawing" at the reins to slow him down and Betty hanging on for dear life.

A short distance from the farm, with barns in sight, total exhaustion took over. Prince skidded to a stop with both front legs splayed out in front of him and his hind legs on the ground—a sitting position unusual for a horse. He was in a lather of sweat and breathing heavily. The two young ladies leapt off not knowing what to do. Frightened from the wild ride, they were even more afraid that poor old Prince was breathing his last breath. But Prince was made of sterner stuff. When his labored breathing returned to normal, he struggled to his feet, shook himself, and walked slowly home with Britta and Betty on either side.

At the Publick House, the former box stalls that existed when Prince was there have become partially enclosed areas for small groups of diners. Our family likes to imagine that people using Prince's former stall have sometimes heard a ghostly neigh and the faint clip clop of horse's hooves, particularly when a distant train whistle is heard.

Britta

RIDING AND DRIVING Prince and helping her family cope with the tasks of running *Oakholm*, was a small part of Britta's life. She was afflicted with a speech defect that never left her. She stammered on both consonants and vowels. This made it difficult for her in school, and it was a problem for her socially as well. As time progressed, she compensated by doing things well with her hands and she became an accomplished hand-weaver. Her interest took her to Sweden where she learned to design textiles. Fishing was a sport she loved. She tied her own flies and cast for bass and trout. Another hobby was archaeology. On a hillside overlooking the lake at *Oakholm*, her careful digging revealed campsites of the Quaboags, the Native American tribe indigenous to the area until the end of King Philip's War in the late 17th century. She uncovered pottery shards, flint arrowheads, and the subtle patterns of baskets in the gravel. Examples of these patterns were lifted out of the soil after being sprayed with a wax compound. They are currently in the collection of Harvard's Peabody Museum and are thought to be two thousand years old. I can see Britta now, her legs dangling into a square hole, digging with a spoon or a small spade and carefully spreading the soil on a sheet to see if any traces of Native American objects might be found.

Britta displaying her weaving at her home, Fencliffe *(1965)*

She looked after her own comfort as well. On one corner of the sheet was always a small picnic basket in which were soft drinks, sandwiches and a cookie.

Britta eventually lived in a house of her own on a small farm called *Fencliffe*, adjacent to *Oakholm*. Most of the sizable farmhouse was built in the 1780s but part dates back to the original log cabin of 1690. It has one massive chimney serving five fireplaces. Three are usable. When Britta took over the place, the pine floors were so worn that they had to be replaced with beautiful wide chestnut boards from the attic. Britta called it her burglar alarm because the floor squeaked loudly when anyone walked on it. The living room is dominated by an antique kitchen fireplace with a bake-oven built into the brick. In the back of the fireplace, as part of the chimney, is a secret room that can be accessed by a closet under the stairway. Britta was convinced that it had been used to hide slaves on their way to freedom in Canada—part of the Underground Railroad prior to Lincoln's Emancipation Proclamation.

Horseback Riding

CHILDHOOD WAS DIFFERENT for us in the 1920s and early 1930s than for youngsters in the first decade of the 21st century. When we were not in school, we were liberated from parental or adult care and supervision for most of the day. This assumed that we had done our chores inside and outside our houses. We walked two miles to Sunday schools. In the city, we took streetcars to movie theaters—the streetcar was ten cents, the movie was ten cents. We brought Mother's lists to stores and returned home with groceries. If it was too far to walk with heavy parcels, we drove a horse and wagon. We were outdoors most of the time, weather permitting. We had time to absorb the natural world—tadpoles, frogs, fishes, cranes, herons, and ducks in the lake and multitudes of birds in woods and fields, as well as animals such as rabbits, woodchucks, squirrels and skunks. With coaching from Mother, we learned about the flowers and trees, and the mushrooms that proliferated under our oak trees.

When *Oakholm* was purchased in 1925 and for several years thereafter, all public roads leading to it were gravel as were all the roads within a radius of ten miles. These made an ideal surface for horseback riding—good firm footing that was easy on the hooves. We rode

Dirt roads leading to the Oakholm *barns (1930)*

for miles on these roads, through woods and fields, along lakes and streams, past busy farms. Brooks were found where horse and rider could drink on hot days. Birch beer and Baby Ruth candy bars were available at country stores for five cents each. Neighbors had horses and ponies too, and we often rode together. Frequently I called the Coes brothers—June and Put—who lived only a mile away or Bill Bennett, a mile and a half. We were on the same party telephone line and could call by cranking each other's numbers. Our number was one long ring and one short one. Calls were often monitored by sneaky neighbors on the same party line who put their receivers to their ears when they heard a neighbor's ring on their telephone. Sometimes you could hear the intruder's heavy breathing. Our calls must have been disappointingly innocent. We would arrange meeting times and picnics with our friends. Rides were a minimum of two hours with plenty of time allowed for food and drink, most of which was purloined from family kitchens and iceboxes. We knew most of our neighbors. We knew the storekeepers in the towns that we rode through. What usually brought us home was the work required of us at our respective farms—cutting brush around fields and roads, hoeing and weeding vegetable gardens, haying, feeding and tending animals. When you add good meals and swimming on hot days and snowshoeing and skiing in winter, it's clear that we led active, healthy lives.

Three of our horses, Daisy, King and Prince have their own chapters in this book. However, over the years *Oakholm* acquired a number of other equine animals that deserve at least some mention so that you can picture them on the lovely country roads and fields and trails carrying us on their backs or pulling wagons, buggies, and sleighs. Important also were those who cared for the horses. Members of the family did their bit to keep their horses fed and clean, but so much of our time was spent in business and distant schools that horsemen were employed to keep horses, stable, and equipment in tip top condition. They also did their share of general farm work.

Thankfully having outgrown Daisy, the terrible Shetland, I became at the age of ten the proud rider and driver of a pair of Welsh ponies, Nip and Tuck. They were dark chestnut with white blazes, exactly the same size and weight, a perfect matched pair. They arrived with harnesses and a two-seat surrey with no "fringe on top." They were

John on Nip, Britta on Tuck (1930)

trained equally well to pull carriages or carry riders. However, in temperament, Nip and Tuck were poles apart. Tuck, the mare, was quiet and gentle but by no means lazy. She was everybody's favorite and a safe ride even for a neophyte. Nip, on the other hand, had an exuberant nature. Riding him required all my attention. He wanted to run. He bucked. He reared. He shied away from imagined enemies. But he was never mean. He never bit or tried to knock me off his back by running under tree branches. I think Nip thought he was giving his rider a good time when he performed his crazy antics. Under control, he was a fine animal to ride with smooth gaits and a good disposition.

Nip and Tuck arrived at about the same time that the new horse barn was finished. They joined the horses previously acquired—Prince and King—as well as Molly and Bess, two large, black Percherons. The barn was a handsome building and I can well remember evening meetings between Father and Harry Fullam, the country contractor. Father sketched the building inside and out, and Fullam drew out its exact dimensions. They had long and friendly arguments about details— where doors and windows should be placed and what size stalls should be; where the saddle and harness room should be located as well as the watering trough; how much space should be allocated for carriages. The finished product—still intact today—provided space for seven horses, four carriages, tack room, feed room, manure pit and two stories of hay storage overhead.

The barn was built in 1930, just after the stock market crash of 1929 and during the early phases of the devastating Depression that followed. Our first horseman was Swen Pulson, who had just graduated as a mechanical engineer from Worcester Polytechnic Institute and was having trouble finding a job in his chosen field.

Swen was my second cousin, liked by the whole family. He hardly knew one end of a horse from the other, but was intelligent enough to quickly learn his new trade. Being eight years younger, I enjoyed helping him care for and exercise the animals. We philosophized quite a bit while riding over the countryside, and I felt that I learned a bit about life from my sophisticated, elderly cousin of twenty-one.

Nip and Tuck eventually proved to be too small for a lad in his early teens. In the nearby town of Grafton, a good home was found for them. They later became famous. Metro-Goldwyn-Mayer filmed part of the movie based on Eugene O'Neill's play, *Ah, Wilderness!*, in Grafton, since it fit O'Neill's description of a typical New England village with its white 18th and 19th century houses, meeting house, inn, and fire house, all of which surrounded the village green and bandstand. Nip and Tuck were featured in several scenes of the movie, pulling a two-seater surrey with a bevy of costumed young beauties therein. We, their previous owners, were very proud of our former ponies and boasted to our friends that their good manners and excellent condition in the film were the result of the care and training they had received at *Oakholm*.

Mother was never enthusiastic about our horses. She didn't ride and would rarely agree to be a passenger in a carriage or sleigh. She was always worried about our joining what she called the "horsey set." In her mind, those who took part in horse shows or hunts were "racey" people who drank to excess and whose behavior was immoral. Father, on the other hand, was always proud of what we owned—be it horses, cows, or paintings. He loved to show them off.

An armed truce was finally established between our parents. We could enter horse shows if the location was within a day's riding distance from the farm. Cattle could be shown anytime anywhere—evidently "cow people" were not considered immoral. The first horse show we attended took place right at *Oakholm*. It was planned by Mother, Father and sister, Britta. Programs were printed, a riding ring was laid out below the tennis court, and a table set up to hold ribbons. Those who entered were neighboring riders and drivers, as well as our family group—about twenty in all.

Everything went as planned. No one fell, although a few animals acted up to the embarrassment of their riders or drivers. The participants wondered why ribbons were not handed out at the conclusion of each class. They were informed that all prizes would be awarded at the end of the show. When that moment finally arrived, Father ordered all the contestants to form a line as he called their names with his megaphone.

Then, with Mother at his side holding a basket of ribbons, he affixed a blue ribbon to the bridle of the first horse. Moving down the line, horse and rider No. 2 also received a blue ribbon. Then No. 3. It soon became apparent that every contestant would receive the top prize. Some felt annoyed, having expected to receive the only blue ribbon in their class, but as time passed, and as the last blue ribbon was awarded to the twentieth horse and rider, everyone joined in the spirit of non-competition. Sporting their blue ribbons, twenty winners paraded up and down the main streets of Brookfield to show what marvelous horses they owned.

Teddy's Choice

SEVERAL YEARS AFTER the disposal of the infected cattle at *Oakholm*, Father was ready to acquire a new herd. Barns, barnyards, and fences had been disinfected. Pastures had been cleansed by two years of sun, wind, rain, and snow. Most importantly, Mother had given her approval. She said, "All right, George, if you must have cows, I insist that each one be tested for tuberculosis before she sets foot on our premises, and after she does arrive, she must be tested again at least once each year. I also want you to make sure that the help you hire to milk the cows and care for them come from disease-free farms as well." Mother's rules anticipated state and federal laws enacted later, but Father and the rest of the family had learned their lesson and were in full accord with her.

We agreed that Father should buy registered Guernseys only. We liked their looks—large, light brown spots on a white background and pink noses. Their size was right, smaller than the black-and-white Holsteins, but larger than the fawn-colored Jerseys. Guernseys were a calm breed with nicely curved horns. Even more important, we liked Guernsey milk better than other varieties. It had a slightly golden color that made it visually appealing, and it had a wonderfully rich flavor.

Father knew very little about acquiring good, pure-bred, registered

Guernsey cattle, but he remembered that Myron Converse, president of the Worcester Five Cents Savings Bank, owned the last dairy farm within the Worcester city limits, and that Myron's cattle were Guernseys. Soon, he and Myron were visiting the great Guernsey farms of Massachusetts and surrounding states.

Langwater Farms in North Easton, Massachusetts, was owned by the Ames family—good Boston Brahmins. Their Guernsey herd was considered one of the best in the country. The original Guernseys in the Langwater herd were imported around the turn of the century by Frederick Lathrop Ames directly from the Isle of Guernsey in the English Channel. The Ames family wealth emanated originally from the Ames Shovel Company, the world's largest manufacturer of hand shovels at the time. Father bought two Langwater cows and a heifer at what he considered to be exorbitant prices. Mr. Ames would not bargain.

Closer to *Oakholm*, the Mixter farm in Hardwick, Massachusetts, also had fine Guernseys. Father bought an additional cow and three heifers. Two members of the Mixter family were renowned surgeons at the Massachusetts General Hospital in Boston. In recent years, Torrance Watkins and Erik Fleming have beautifully restored the Mixter farm buildings. Some of the country's finest hunters—horses, not people— are now housed and trained there.

Having acquired cows with the right conformations, milk producing genes and pedigrees, it was time to buy a bull that would produce champion progeny. In the 1920s it was necessary to own a bull for breeding purposes on your own farm, because reliable methods of artificial insemination had not yet been developed. Father and Myron

Teddy's Choice of Hillstead being led by the nose (1930)

Converse searched far and wide, and eventually found a bull provoca-
tively named "Teddy's Choice of Hillstead" at the *Hillstead Farms* in
Pennsylvania. He was a half-brother to the reigning world-champion
Guernsey cow. Teddy's Choice was a massive, bad-tempered brute who
arrived at *Oakholm* in the summer of 1927. As he came down the truck
ramp, he set four large cloven hooves on the soil of his new home, and
snorted and bellowed loudly, as if to say, "I will do everything I can to
make life miserable for my new owners."

Teddy was big for a Guernsey bull, and difficult to handle even with
the "bull pole" that traveled with him from Pennsylvania. This clever
device consisted of a cable mechanism strung through five feet of steel

tubing that had a handle at one end and a hook at the other attached to Teddy's nose ring. Using this bull pole, a handler could lead, halt, or back him up and thereby prevent him from getting too close.

Kept in a shed with a yard of his own, Teddy was led out to meet the lady members of the herd at proper times. Teddy's Choice became the sire of a number of fine heifers produced by the Langwater and Mixter cows. We kept only the females. The bulls were immediately sold. Mother named the first three heifers after the Three Graces: Hulda, Anna Skoog, and Anna Nygren. Needless to say, the human "Annas" were not thrilled to have cow namesakes. But when the animals became prize Guernseys, their dismay gave way to pride.

Unfortunately, Teddy's Choice became increasingly difficult to handle. One day, with a toss of his head, he pulled the bull pole out of the hands of the elderly Will Pike, and then attacked and gored him. Luckily the wound was not fatal. Nonetheless, Teddy's Choice was immediately butchered before he could commit any more mayhem. He had the last laugh, however. His meat was too tough to cut, let alone chew. When we ground it into hamburger, even Ned, our German shepherd, and Billie, our Welsh terrier, refused to eat it.

Milking

WHEN I FIRST ARRIVED at *Oakholm* as a small boy of eight, I thought I knew a lot about everything, but it didn't take long for me to realize that I was a real rube. When our boss farmer told me that I should brush the hens' teeth at dawn the next morning, I carefully laid out my toothbrush the night before in preparation. I also thought it would take no time at all to learn to milk a cow. In those days, milking was done by hand. I learned quickly that hens had no teeth, but milking a cow was a different matter. At 5:30 a.m., I watched Stellan Peterson and his hired man, Ernie, setting up their round, three-legged steel milking stools, each about eighteen inches high. They were positioned just to the right of the cow and directly under the cow's udder. Large, clean, stainless steel milking pails were held firmly between the lower legs of the milkers. Next, two of the cow's teats were firmly grasped in the bare hands of each milker, and milk was directed from cow to pail by a squeezing and pulling motion of the milker's hands. The stream of milk this produced made a satisfying sound as it hit the sides and bottom of the steel pail. This looked easy to me. I was handed a stool and pail by Stellan, which I promptly placed under the cow's right side. When I first sat on the stool I fell over. I tried again, this time grasping two of the cow's

Stellan Peterson with a fine Guernsey cow (1930)

teats, and pulled them in what I thought was the correct manner. But no milk came. Hulda—the cow I was attempting to milk—was visibly annoyed, and swished the end of her rough tail across my face, making me tip over again, overturning the empty pail. After a good laugh, Stellan and Ernie took pity on me. They told me how to hold the cow's tail under my left knee using just enough pressure between my calf and thigh as I sat on the stool. They showed me that you didn't just pull the cow's teat to produce a stream of milk, you pulled and squeezed with each finger, from forefinger to little finger in succession. This caused the milk to flow in a steady stream from cow to pail, sort of like playing a scale on a violin. This was not so easy for an eight-year old. It took me several weeks to become proficient. Much to my gratification, Stellan told me that there were those who never learned to milk properly without annoying the cow, who could easily withhold her milk.

The production of each purebred Guernsey cow was weighed every day to determine her annual output. We had a few animals that produced more than twelve thousand pounds annually—or about six thousand quarts. A high producer with good conformation became a very valuable animal. Her calves were sought after as well, especially if they had an excellent sire.

I always enjoyed showing my city friends how cows were milked. I would usher them into the barn and take them to a spot behind the cow that Stellan was milking. He would say, "Hello," and, at that moment, direct a stream of warm milk to the face of the nearest visitor by squeezing and aiming the cow's teat. This always brought forth whoops and guffaws from everyone present.

Making Hay

HAY WAS THE MAIN field crop at *Oakholm*. The mix of timothy, red top, orchard grass, oats, alfalfa and clover was an essential part of the diet of the horses and cows. Not only was it nutritious for the animals, but it also provided bulk to keep their digestive systems in order. In the fall, fields were plowed which turned over the old weedy turf to a depth of about ten to fourteen inches. Molly and Bess pulled the plow. Stellan walked behind, simultaneously holding the reins and keeping a hand on each of the long handles to keep the plow upright and pitched correctly. Next came the harrowing, which smoothed over the plowed fields, making them ready for planting. The harrow consisted of a series of disks, which rotated as the machine was pulled along by the horses, cutting up the rows of heavy turf previously turned over by the plow.

In order to sweeten the typically acidic soil of New England, the horses pulled a spreader that distributed pulverized limestone across the field. The lime in the eight-foot wide container of the spreader was let out in a fine, eight-foot stream from the V-shaped bottom which ensured an even distribution of the material.

Next came the horse and cow manure. The horse-drawn manure spreader was an ingenious mechanism. It was in the shape of a wagon

Stellan Peterson haying with horses, Molly and Bess (1932)

with a seat in front. A belt of steel links and wooden slats ran over the wagon bottom, bringing the manure to the back where rotating teeth picked up the manure, broke it up and spun it into a cloud over the field. As it sprayed its load on the field, it also produced an amazingly pungent aroma which could be detected for miles. In local parlance, the spreader was called the "honey wagon." Occasionally we used chemical fertilizer if there was insufficient manure available or if tests showed that it was necessary.

We seeded the soil in the spring using yet another ingenious horse-drawn contraption similar to the lime spreader. This had mechanical attachments along the bottom which formed shallow grooves in the earth. It then released the seed and covered it with soil. Small areas were seeded by hand. Seeding was usually done in late March or early April in Brookfield—although, in some cases, we planted winter rye in the fall and plowed and harrowed in the spring. Rotting rye provided nitrogen and fiber to the earth. It also prevented soil erosion on hilly terrain. In order to keep the hayfields from being overrun, farm hands—armed with axes, saws, brush hooks, and clippers—pruned and cut brush and trees along the edges of each field.

After planting, we waited expectantly to see the seeds sprout in the dark brown earth. A solid greening of the fields meant that seventy-five percent or more of the seed had germinated. This was known as a very good "catch" and required the right combination of sun and rain.

We all became weather forecasters in spring and summer. East and northeast winds produced rains and storms. With southeast breezes and muggy air came afternoon thunderstorms. Rapid temperature changes up or down often preceded unsettled weather. West and northwest breezes usually brought the finest days, sunny and clear. Big fluffy cumulus clouds were with us during fair weather, but could sometimes develop into brief afternoon showers. The cloud lines of a "mackerel" sky portended rain. Then there was the moon which had a definite effect on the weather in its various phases. Sunsets and sunrises told meteorological stories as well:

> *Red sky in the morning*
> *Sailors take warning.*
> *Red sky at night*
> *Sailors delight.*

Lounging on my back in the grass on a beautiful summer day, looking up at the sky, seeing castles, mountains, faces, and animals in the strange and wonderful cloud formations provided peaceful moments of my boyhood at *Oakholm*. Such times were rare amid all the chores we had to do on the farm.

We cut the first hay crop in early June. Molly and Bess, as usual, did most of the work. They pulled a sickle bar mower that cut an eight-foot swath through the hayfield, leaving even rows of freshly mown hay. The faster the hay dried, the better the food value. Thorough drying also lessened the risk of a fire in the barns. Even a small amount of wet hay stacked in a barn could spontaneously combust with disastrous results.

The flat hay left by the cutter was tossed off the ground and fluffed up by another unusual machine—an eight-foot wide tedder. A series of two-tined forks attached to a shaft between the tedder's wheels swept up the hay and literally threw it up in the air. The hay fell in irregular patterns, making it easier for breezes to blow through the piles and dry them faster. Tedding was sometimes done two or three times to get the hay thoroughly dry.

With luck and good weather, the hay was usually ready in three days for its trip to the barn. Raking was next, a one-horse operation. The horse-drawn rake was about eight-feet in width, with a mechanism that held about sixteen steel tines. These were a half-circle in shape, and made of spring steel so that they wouldn't break as they raked up the hay over uneven ground or embedded rocks. The youngest member of the work force always had the raking job. I was more than proud, at the age of twelve, to sit in the steel seat at the center of the rake and drive Prince over the hay fields. When the rake was full, I used a foot-activated treadle to lift the rake and let the hay out. The trick was to form even rows.

Next, the hay was pitch-forked into rounded piles. These were called "hay cocks," and they needed to be just the right size and weight to be pitched onto the hay wagon with a three-tined fork with a long handle.

Pitching these fifty-pound plus hay cocks eight feet to the top of a load for several afternoon hours on a hot summer day was work for only powerful, robust men. Mother, Betty, and Britta, along with the "Annas," came out at intervals to refresh the workers with cold drinks—usually a concoction of sweetened rhubarb syrup in cold water. We still drink it with great relish. It's even better than fresh lemonade.

Each wagon load was ten-feet tall, ten-feet wide, and twelve-feet long. That was about all the horses could pull. Backing the wagon into the barn took considerable skill on the part of Ernie Mundell, our cheerful hired man. Once the wagon was in the barn, a large fork lifted the hay out. The fork was attached to a heavy rope that ran through a pulley system that was attached to Bess, our strongest horse. The fork dropped the hay on a platform, and workers then pushed the hay to various storage areas in the barn. Working in one hundred degree temperatures on that platform was not the easiest job either.

The most crucial job belonged to the man on the hay wagon. He directed the men to pitch the hay so that the hay was both loaded evenly and each forkful was interlaced neatly with the one above and below it. The wagon had no sidewalls, which made it easier to pitch the hay on board, but harder to keep it there. Hay on a badly loaded wagon could easily slide off, so this final stage of harvesting got lots of attention.

When I was fifteen, I got my first chance to oversee the loading of the hay. All went well at first. The mammoth load was ready for the barn. Standing ten-feet high on top of the load, I proudly gave the signal to Molly and Bess to head for the barn. Our route lay over a field on a side hill, and I noticed with dismay that the load was beginning to slide ominously to the left. I swung the horses to the right to try to prevent the inevitable, but to no avail. Ten feet of hay—with me on top—slid off the wagon, earning me some loud Bronx cheers from my fellow workers.

The punishment for losing a load was simple but effective. I had to pitch all the fallen hay back on the wagon by myself while my fellow "haymakers" sat in the shade making a chorus of derisive comments.

A full hay wagon after tractors came along (1932)

Mother's Birthday

ON JUNE 23, 1929 AT SIX O'CLOCK in the morning, Father awakened me. He tapped his left hand on my shoulder and put his finger to his lips, signaling silence. Right away I knew that he was organizing the troops—my two sisters and me and the Three Graces (the two Annas and Hulda)—for the annual parade to Mother's bedside. Each of us received our orders. Britta went out to pick fresh wildflowers. Betty, only four, was given a wooden spoon and a tin plate to bang. The two Annas and Hulda set up hot coffee and fresh-baked Swedish coffee bread on a tray. I picked a bowl of sweet wild strawberries. Father located his tall silk hat and his cornet and we all gathered at the bottom of the stairs. We were a strange and wondrous group, dressed in outlandish ways. We wore funny hats, sashes, boots, and robes. We decorated our faces with mustaches and elaborate designs drawn with charcoal. It took us an hour to prepare. At seven sharp the parade began—Father played a Finnish march on his horn while the rest of us beat time on pots and pans and sang. Gammy, the Cairn terrier, and Billie, the Welsh terrier, barked at the rear of the parade.

If you think we surprised Mother, think again. When we burst through the bedroom door, she was wearing her best silk nightie with

*The Jeppson family, from left, Britta, GNJ, Betty, SUJ, and John
(1928)*

a beautiful pink shawl around her shoulders. Her long, brown, shiny hair was done to perfection. Even the bed was smooth and unwrinkled. Mother showed her appreciation with hugs and kisses for everyone. Being a bashful lad of thirteen, I avoided as much of the show of affection as possible and was delighted when, at last, we were able to attack the food and drink.

The morning festivities were just the beginning. Mother's birthday was two days after the summer solstice, the longest day of the year. In Scandinavian countries, it is traditionally a day of great celebration dating back to pagan times. People of the north still revel on the one day of the year when daylight lasts twenty-four hours. They sing and dance around maypoles. They feast on mountains of boiled crayfish and drink *aquavit* ("water of life" in Swedish), a potent potato-based alcoholic beverage, to the accompaniment of rousing songs. Bonfires are always part of the scene.

We did likewise on Mother's birthday, and spent the day preparing for the evening. A twenty-foot wooden maypole was hammered together with two cross arms attached and put up on the lawn at the lakeside. We covered the pole with fresh-cut birch boughs and armloads of wild daisies. Four wreaths, three feet in diameter, were similarly decorated and hung from the cross arms of the maypole.

As the deadline of 6:00 p.m. approached, the family dressed up in lovely Swedish peasant costumes. I was forced to wear a boy's costume from Dalarna, a Swedish province. The outfit included a red skullcap, a white shirt, an embroidered red vest, yellow knee pants, red stockings, and black shoes with silver buckles. I hated the outfit, particularly when the ladies said, "You look so cute, John!"

Olaf Lundstrom, an accordion player, knew all the Swedish dance tunes—polkas, *hambos*, and *schottisches*. The guests wound their way down the hill to the maypole where tables and benches had been placed. Olaf and a few others were dressed in costume as well. Everything began at the same moment. Olaf started to play and couples began their athletic dancing. Some made a beeline for the *smörgåsbord*—a wonderful collection of Scandinavian delicacies, such as smoked salmon and sill salad—potatoes, pickled herring, hard-boiled eggs, all cut up and covered with dill sauce. There was also a variety of cold meats, sausages, meatballs, and various other salads. Other guests gravitated toward the drinks, especially the beer and *aquavit*.

Father got everyone's attention by blowing *Reveille* on his trumpet so he could announce the schedule of events. First off was a drink, this was a prerequisite for a dance around the maypole. We danced a *hambo*, which is a vigorous, high-stepping example of terpsichorean art done properly by very few of the guests—but attempted by all. After the *hambo* came the food and toasts to my mother the birthday child. Next Britta and I brought the enormous birthday cake around the corner of the boathouse with forty-one lighted candles on it. We carried it on the family cake board, which had fifty holes around the edge in which to place five-inch candles. Everyone sang "Happy Birthday" with gusto. This was followed by an even louder Swedish rendition of "Ja må hon leva." The lyrics of the song translate in English to "May she live, may she live, for one hundred years! Hurrah! Hurrah! Hurrah!"

That was the end of Mother's birthday program. However, the dancing and drinking went on and on. My sisters and I were conscious of romantic couples drifting into secret places amongst the groves and fields of *Oakholm*.

YOU WHO READ these stories will wonder why there are so many references to people and things Swedish. My parents were born in the United States but their mothers and fathers were Swedish, and immigrated here in the 1880s. My mother's parents moved back to Sweden after producing five children in Worcester, Massachusetts. Mother came back to marry Father after living in Sweden for ten years. My wife Marianne's mother was born in Sweden and lived there until she married her American fiancée. As a result of all the immigrations, moves, and marriages, my sisters and I had one set of grandparents, three uncles and aunts and nine first cousins in Sweden, whereas Marianne had one aunt, one uncle, and four cousins who lived there as well. All these relatives have kept in touch with each other to a greater or lesser degree. Quite a few have visited us and we them. Father took his engineering degree at the Royal School of Mines in Stockholm and several cousins have attended universities in the U.S.A. We are proud of our Swedish roots, but more proud to be citizens of this great country of ours, which gave our family so many wonderful opportunities.

Betty in Swedish costume, age two (1927)

Gardens

Mother's major contribution to *Oakholm* was the gardens. As a child, she lived in a house next to the Green estate in Worcester, where there were extensive formal gardens in which she played. The Green estate eventually became the city's largest park, containing a golf course, fishponds, war memorials, and gardens. Worcester may have been the source of Mother's love of horticulture, but it was back in Sweden that she really learned the botanical craft. Although born in Worcester, she returned to Sweden as a twelve-year old with her parents and siblings because her father was offered a better job than he had in Worcester. Due to the influence of the great naturalist and botanist Carl Linnaeus, all Swedish schoolchildren were required to study botany. When she moved back to the United States at the age of twenty-two, she had acquired a deep knowledge of plants.

At 41 Burncoat Street, my parents' first home, Mother designed and planted a large and beautiful garden. When we moved to Drury Lane and when we purchased *Oakholm*, Mother took on the simultaneous development of two major gardens. At *Oakholm*, she planted a magnificent border of rhododendrons and azaleas along the entire four-hundred foot entrance drive. Still flourishing today, some of the individual specimens

SUJ in her garden at 41 Burncoat Street with Britta and John (1924)

are over fourteen feet tall. The azaleas include several varieties, which bloom successively over the spring months. Down the hill on the northeast side of the main house, Mother created a rock garden that was bisected by a serpentine fieldstone path with large stones placed naturalistically on each side. The stones were found elsewhere on the farm and dragged to the site on a "stone boat" by Molly and Bess, the Percheron workhorses.

The banking on one side of the tennis court is now covered entirely with Scottish heather. The extensive area of groundcover has developed from two tiny plants smuggled from Sweden by Mother in 1930. The climate and soil in southern and central Sweden are very similar to that of central Scotland. Both countries have large, rocky hillsides covered by the same variety of heather. The soil, topography, and climate of

Central Massachusetts are similarly amenable to growing heather.

Mother's horticultural handiwork is probably most evident in the lovely terrace garden near the main house. It features many perennials that she planted originally at Burncoat Street, and moved later to Drury Lane, and finally to *Oakholm*. Some of the shrubs in the front of the house made the same journey. Mother left much that is beautiful surrounding us. In addition to her garden, she developed an extensive library of books on a wide variety of nature subjects.

Mother and Father's marriage was certainly a happy one. The only marital battles that I can remember were about trees. Father liked to clear land and preferred sunshine to shade around buildings. Mother never wanted any healthy tree to be removed, no matter where it grew. The arguments were never violent, but I do remember a few times when Mother tearfully ran up the stairs to her bedroom, slamming the door behind her. When this happened, Father knew he was licked. The tree "at risk" was saved.

Mother would have been delighted to know that her love of horticulture still flourishes in succeeding generations of her family. Her granddaughter, Ingrid, has a master's degree in botany and is an accomplished garden designer. Another granddaughter, Muffy is embellishing her country place, *Timberock*, adjacent to *Oakholm*, with new shrubs, flowers, and fruit trees. And in 1989, at the age of seventy-four, I became the oldest person at that time to pass the Master Gardener's course in Massachusetts. Additionally, I have been restoring, maintaining, and adding to Mother's gardens ever since. They have been featured several times on garden tours organized by the Worcester County Horticultural Society, which owns and operates Tower Hill Botanic

Garden in Boylston, Massachusetts. At this horticultural showplace, which includes 132 acres of gardens, meadows, and woods, there is a terrace overlooking the Lawn Garden named in Mother's honor.

The terrace garden at Oakholm *(2006)*

Thomas Jefferson Bird

ONE EARLY SUMMER MORNING, Mother was wandering around her terrace weeding, deadheading flowers, and doing all the good things that good gardeners do to maintain the beauty of their gardens. At a certain moment, she saw something small moving between a couple of oriental lilies. It was the tiniest of birds—a baby hummingbird—that had fallen out of its nest. Mother could not find the nest to put the baby bird back, nor could any of the rest of us. She took it into the house, placed it in a little open box on a bed of cotton and fed it sugar water syrup with an eyedropper. She fed the tiny bird several times a day and even added a drop of cod-liver oil to give it the vitamins it needed.

Despite the pessimism of the rest of the family, the baby bird flourished under Mother's ministrations. In a short time he was fluttering his wings and in matter of a few weeks was taking his first flights. Mother had placed him in her upstairs porch where she kept a number of houseplants, believing he would fly from plant to plant. This is exactly what he did. You will have noticed that I have changed the pronoun from "it" to "he." It was soon apparent that he fit the description of a male ruby-throated hummingbird.

The entire house became his aviary. Soon the humming noise

from the incredibly fast beating of his wings was heard in every room. Mother encouraged him to fly outside, hoping that he would eventually join his wild siblings. He would not stay out. He fluttered at the doorways until he was let in again. He became a genuine member of the family—he probably realized that most of us were birdbrains just like him. During the cocktail hour, he perched on the rims of our glasses, and was discerning about what he drank. Martinis and whiskey were out, but he enjoyed sips of daiquiris and orange blossoms, after which he flew somewhat erratically.

Mother called him "Perky," a rather common, even inane, name. We talked about it on July Fourth, and decided that he deserved a far more distinguished appellation. Someone remarked on the fact that John Adams and Thomas Jefferson had both died on the Fourth of July, and that our bird should be named after one or the other. Since there were already two Johns in the family, he was christened Thomas Jefferson Bird. The ceremony was quite formal with proper toasts. However, our stuffy Lutheran minister refused to give him a church baptism, so we had to make do with an unconsecrated Jeppson at home.

Late summer arrived, the time when hummingbirds head south, flying more than two thousand miles to Central America. It is hard to imagine that these smallest of birds, whose wings beat in milliseconds, can fly to the Gulf coast of Florida, over the Gulf of Mexico to Costa Rica, Honduras, Nicaragua, and Panama, and then return to our neighborhood in spring. The call of the wild eventually reached Thomas Jefferson Bird, and on one of the occasions when Mother let him outside, he failed to return to the house. We all wished him Godspeed on his journey, never dreaming that we would see him again.

But the following spring on a lovely morning, a handsome, male ruby-throated hummingbird hovered around the door of our screened porch until my mother opened it. In he flew, exploring several rooms, before darting out when she opened the door again. It was obviously Thomas Jefferson Bird checking out his old home. It did not take him long to decide that indoor living was not for him. But he and his descendants have hovered around us ever since, preferring the nectar of our flowers to the gin in our martinis.

A Princely Visit
_____

THE THREE HUNDREDTH ANNIVERSARY of the landing of the first
Swedish colony in America was celebrated in the summer of 1938.
Crossing the Atlantic on three ships, the colonists landed on a point
of land that is now within the present city limits of Wilmington,
Delaware. Control and administration of the Colony was soon taken
over by the New York Dutch, later by the British, and finally by the state
of Delaware. Though not initially successful politically on American
shores, the Swedish colonists and their descendants flourished as farmers, industrialists, and statesmen.

The Crown Prince of Sweden, who later became King Gustaf Adolf
VI, and his wife, Louise, were scheduled to lead a delegation of important Swedes to the United States to take part in a whole series of
ceremonies and festivities, marking the first landing of the Swedes. The
prince made the trip on the *Kungsholm*, but he did not come ashore in
Delaware due to a serious illness. He turned over his duties to his son,
Prince Bertil, then twenty-six years of age. On short notice, Bertil did
a credible job. He was tall and good-looking and spoke English well.

On June 11, 1938, he visited Worcester, home to thirty thousand
Swedes, one of the largest populations in the country. As one of the

leading Swedish-Amercans in Worcester County, Father had arranged the Prince's schedule that included lunch at the Worcester Country Club and visits to the Worcester Art Museum and the Norton Company.

The prince attended a baseball game between the Norton team and that of SKF, the Swedish ball bearing manufacturer. After Father's introduction, Bertil threw out the first ball and said a few words to the assembled crowd around him. Just as he stepped up to the microphone, the heavens opened—lightning flashed and a heavy rain began to pour. Father grabbed someone else's umbrella to hold over the Prince's head. An enterprising photographer captured that precise moment. Thoroughly soaked, Bertil and his three aides were whisked out to Brookfield and *Oakholm* by my father who was drenched as well. There he was scheduled to have a two-hour rest before meeting a group of prominent local citizens and their spouses who had been invited for cocktails and dinner at 6:30 p.m.

The guests arrived promptly, resplendent in gowns and formal dress. Fifteen minutes went by, then thirty, then forty and still no prince. One of the guests, a former singer of lieder and oratorios, took over the piano and sang sad, ancient, unlovely songs in a loud, hollow contralto voice. We are sure the racket kept Bertil in his upstairs room for another quarter of an hour. At last our prince made a gracious entrance, went the rounds of guests and apologized for his tardiness.

His excuses were understandable. Before coming to Worcester and *Oakholm*, he had been given a day of rest from his arduous schedule. This took place at the Vanderbilt estate in Newport, Rhode Island, where he spent his time lounging around a swimming pool with a few friends. But Bertil fell asleep beside the pool, and soon over-exposed his

IT DID RAIN

The return from the Athletic Field was during torrential rain, but the Prince smiles a greeting to the drenched throng while Mr. Jeppson makes good use of the umbrella.

Prince Bertil of Sweden and GNJ holding umbrella (1938)
From the *Worcester Telegram*

fair Scandinavian skin to our hot July sun. Nobody dared to wake him, and his back was badly burned. To his credit, he carried on his daytime activities in Worcester with good grace even though he was in considerable pain. By the time he reached *Oakholm*, however, he needed to relax. What he really wanted to do was sit in seclusion and have his burning body attended to.

At this point, one of his aides found his way to the kitchen to ask for some hot coffee and a bun for his majesty. The Three Graces—Anna Skoog, Anna Nygren, and Hulda—were well prepared for such an eventuality. Fresh coffee, home made gingersnaps and Swedish coffee bread were ready. Anna Nygren was chosen to take the tray with its delicacies to Prince Bertil and his entourage. Up the stairs she marched in her white starched uniform, and knocked on the door. She entered the room after the Prince himself said, "Come in, come in!" She took a couple of steps forward before looking up. On seeing the Prince, she gasped. There he stood in the altogether. Her tray would have crashed to the ground, if Bertil had not caught it with a flourish. Anna immediately turned and ran, never stopping until she reached the safety of the kitchen again. From then on she had a story that she never failed to tell any and all. She became the envy of all her friends.

By the time Bertil put in his reluctant, but gracious, appearance, a number of guests had become unusually loquacious and friendly. They were exceptionally effusive when greeting the aching prince. One of the ladies lost her balance while curtseying. There were those that surmised that the Manhattans, which had been appearing regularly for an hour and a half, may have softened the serious demeanors of many guests that night.

Since the royal visit occurred just a week after July Fourth, the menu consisted of traditional Independence Day fare, poached Atlantic salmon and fresh peas, topped off with a dessert of ice cream and blueberries. After dinner, Bertil and his staff were driven to the Brookfield station where a private railroad car was waiting to take them to New York. Alas, the station no longer exists and no trains stop in Brookfield these days—for princes or anyone else.

The Hurricane of 1938

TODAY, I FIND MYSELF in the parlor of *Oakholm's* main house, looking south into the oak woods and then looking east at the view over Lake Quaboag. It is raining heavily and two inches have fallen since yesterday afternoon. One large dead branch on the great red oak just outside the front door has fallen, breaking because of the weight of rainwater absorbed. Happily, it did no damage as it crashed to the ground, missing the house only by inches. The rain is the tail-end of Hurricane Frances, which did so much damage to the Caribbean islands and to Florida and the Carolinas. I have turned on the noon news on the television to hear the weather forecaster's description of Ivan, a Category 5 hurricane, which again is threatening our southern states.

All this brings back memories of the massive hurricane of 1938, which devastated large areas of New York, Connecticut, Rhode Island, and Massachusetts on September 21 of that year. This storm was extremely unusual in that its forward speed approached seventy miles per hour. This allowed the hurricane to travel far before it had a chance to weaken over cooler waters. The hurricane was forecast by the U.S. National Weather Service to head out into the Atlantic Ocean but instead continued almost due north. It made landfall on Long Island,

New York as a strong Category 3 hurricane on the present-day Saffir-Simpson Hurricane Scale. It then traveled across Long Island Sound into Connecticut, Rhode Island, Massachusetts, New Hampshire, Vermont, and finally into Canada while still moving at an unusually high speed.

On that day Father and I were returning from Cambridge, Massachusetts, where I had been interviewed by two Harvard Business School professors prior to admittance. The wind was brisk and the sky was blue, but as we neared Worcester, our car, a heavy Cadillac, required more and more steering effort to keep it on course. Our route took us up Shrewsbury Street and down steep Belmont Hill to Lincoln Square. We were forced to dodge the fallen maple trees, which lined the streets. We finally reached our house at Drury Lane after circumventing a large fallen tree by driving over granite curbs at Institute Park. We drove straight into the garage, which fortunately had been left open. Sliding the doors shut, we hurried to the side door of the house, hardly able to make any headway against the wind and rain. Objects hurtled through the air narrowly missing us.

My mother and two sisters greeted us with relief. They knew no more than Father and I did about the extent and intensity of the storm. We checked windows and doors. The sounds outside grew louder and louder—windows rattled, branches hit the doors and roof. Father decided to check on the status of the roof through a hatch in the rooftop. We hauled a stepladder up to the attic and placed it directly under the hatch. Father insisted on taking the first peek outside while I steadied the ladder. He unlocked the hatch, which flew open with a great bang. As he stuck his head and shoulders outside, the tremendous force of the wind began to pull him out. I grabbed him around the legs and pulled him down out of harm's way. The two of us got the hatch closed again with great difficulty.

The house was roofed with heavy, graduated slate shingles, each of which weighed a couple of pounds. Fifty or sixty of these were whipped off the roof by the 125 mile per hour wind. Many landed perpendicularly on the front lawn, forming an ancient-looking miniature graveyard. Had we been hit by these "missiles," we would have been sliced in two.

We anxiously waited out the hurricane patrolling the house, checking the windows and assessing the damage outside. Trees lost branches and many were uprooted. News of what was happening elsewhere was slow in coming. There was, of course, no television at that time. Telephone lines were severed everywhere by falling trees. For days, radio was our only link to the outside world. We received news only from transmitters beyond the area hit by the storm, because all the local radio towers had been blown down. Station KDKA in Pittsburgh, Pennsylvania, was for many days the only station that we could get on our radio.

Naturally, we were very worried about what had happened at *Oakholm*. Although only twenty-two miles away, downed trees and wires made it impossible to contact our farm family, the Petersons. We would eventually learn that the water damage was extensive. Fourteen inches in less than twenty-four hours had caused a dam in the North Brookfield reservoir to break. The water poured into Brooks Pond and Lake Lashaway in East Brookfield. The accumulation of waters in these lakes broke through their dams as well creating a tremendous wall of water that roared into Lake Quaboag, raising the water level eleven feet higher than normal. The water rose to the eaves of our lakeside building,

Devastation of forests around Oakholm *(1938)*

the *J House,* used for family gatherings. The high-water mark on its inner walls can still be shown to "Doubting Thomases." The house would have floated away, but fortunately it was anchored by the brick chimney and fireplace. The flowing waters covered marshes and fields, doubling Lake Quaboag's size from five hundred to one thousand acres.

On the third day after the storm, public highways were sufficiently cleared of fallen trees and debris for Father and me to drive out to Brookfield. We were not able to reach the farm by car because of Lake Quaboag's floodwaters. We borrowed a flat-bottomed boat, and rowed a quarter mile to the road leading to *Oakholm.* We then walked about a mile picking our way over fallen trees to the farm. There, the Petersons joyfully greeted us. They were just about to eat their noonday meal to which we were cordially invited. They were cooking over an open fire—a roast chicken from the farm flock, boiled carrots, potatoes, fresh lettuce and tomatoes from the garden—wonderful stuff, particularly when topped off with juicy apples from one of our trees.

Stellan Peterson, who would be our boss farmer for fifty years, was a strong man and a good problem solver. Since there was no electricity, he cooled and preserved the milk from our twenty cows in the icehouse. Since the electric water pump in the artesian well could not operate, he dug out a spring for drinking water. He moved fences to permit the cows to drink water out of the brook, and he used axe and saw to remove trees and branches from roofs, driveways, and entrances to barns and houses. All these tasks were accomplished soon after the storm ended, including killing a chicken for our lunch.

At *Oakholm*, we tramped around the fields and forests. The destruction was unbelievable. Every major tree was uprooted or broken beyond repair. Branches torn from trees covered most of the open land. The high water added to the general devastation. "Mother's Cathedral," a grove of one-hundred foot, century-old white pines, with three-to-four foot diameter trunks, was no more. Only small trees and saplings remained standing. They were flexible enough to bend and weave when hit by the powerful gusts of wind.

The question before us was, "What do we do now?" After viewing the damage, the three of us, Father, Stellan, and I, sat down wearily on a couple of fallen oaks to hold a palaver. Our "democratic" discussion resulted in the following decisions—all made by Father:

First, put up a sawmill. It took two weeks to find an old clunker in Belchertown that Stellan repaired and put in working order in a field near the farmhouse. This involved building a shed over it as well.

Cleaning up fallen trees (1938)

Second, hire the equivalent of six men full time, proficient with axe and saw to clean up the forest and run the sawmill. We were still in the Great Depression, and labor was plentiful. Actually, twelve part-timers were hired, most of them from the Norton Company, where Father was works manager. The company employed its people half time to keep them on the payroll in those difficult times. Passenger trains from Worcester stopped in Brookfield, providing the men with good transportation—better even than what we have today.

Third, buy a generator operated by diesel oil or gasoline, to provide electricity for pumps, stoves, coolers, refrigerators, and lights. We realized that having our own source of power in the event of storms or accidents was necessary. A generator was installed within a month.

Oakholm became a beehive of activity. Men sawed logs from the fallen trees, which were pulled by horses to the sawmill. They stacked the lumber by hand in piles adjacent to the mill, separating it by type of wood—oak, maple, white pine, cherry, and ash—and slanting it so that water, rain, and snow could run off. Planks were stacked by size. The men threw branches, ripped from trees and cut from logs, into great piles out on the hay fields. The piles were burned in the winter when snow kept the fires from spreading. The work crew sawed the large-diameter branches in short lengths and later split them for firewood. They cleared one area of broken trees so thoroughly that it was eventually used as a field for growing hay or corn. In order to remove stumps—this was before bulldozers were widely available—the men used dynamite to literally blow them out of the ground. Pieces of stump, stones, and mud flew up and outward in a spectacular pattern with each explosion. Family and friends enjoyed watching from a safe distance.

Hurricane lumber was a drug on the market. It was practically given away. Father said, "We're not going to sell it until times are better." Too much time and effort had gone into it to give it away, and he didn't sell it until 1941—when the economy began to recover just before the the United States entered World War II. He got a good price.

At *Oakholm*, the saplings and trees that survived the hurricane of 1938 are the giants of today. Nearly seventy-five years old now, these great specimens of white pine, oak, maple and birch are spread throughout the property—some close to the family homestead and farm buildings, many others scattered throughout the surrounding woods. In one large white pine, American bald eagles have taken up residence in a huge nest seventy feet above the ground.

If *Oakholm* were visited again by a storm as powerful as the hurricane of 1938, the great trees now closely surrounding our houses and barns would come crashing down on our roofs and walls. Piles of rubble would be left—soon covered by vines and brush—a paradise for birds, bats, and chipmunks. Perhaps years later, archeologists may find some cracked skulls and bones where our family once held sway.

Love In Bloom

Marianne Shellabarger Jeppson (1943)

MARIANNE'S FAMILY, THE SHELLABARGERS, and my family, the Jeppsons, had known each other several years before we were born. But it was not until 1929 that she and I were brought together at *Oakholm*. Marianne was nine, her sister Ingrid was twelve, and I was thirteen.

While our respective mothers were enjoying each other's company and reminiscing, it was my responsibility to keep the Shellabarger sisters occupied. They particularly liked to swim. Since Lake Quaboag's shore was two hundred feet from the house and the day they arrived was sunny and hot, they could not wait to don their swimsuits and jump in the water with me close behind. At nine, Marianne was pretty, but had not yet matured to the beauty she later became. On the other hand, Ingrid at twelve looked like a combination of Ingrid Bergman and Venus di Milo. To show off my manly strength and endurance, I suggested that we swim across the lake, a distance of a mile and a quarter. I never thought they would take me up on it. We set out at a speed that I thought would soon tire them. It didn't. They kept it up all the way, reaching the other side of the lake two hundred yards ahead of me. After a short rest, I told them we would now walk back. The Shellabarger girls would not hear of it. They dove back into the water and swam across the lake again while I walked the six miles of shoreline to meet them.

Tennis was another ego deflator for me. Ingrid played like Helen Wills Moody—at that time the reigning world champion. Even Marianne at her tender age could keep up with me on the court, until she sprained her ankle. Horseback riding was the only sport in which I could surpass the two sisters, mainly because I had been at it much longer than they. After all, I had owned a horse for five years.

My next meeting with Ingrid and Marianne was in Williamstown, Massachusetts, at Marshall Brown's farm, which the Shellabargers leased for the summer of 1932. I'm convinced that my mother and Vifvan Shellabarger were beginning to foist a low-key matchmaking program on Ingrid and me who were then fifteen and sixteen. Unfortunately, tennis and dancing occupied most of the weekend. My ability to swim and play tennis was limited, but as a ballroom dancer, I was in a league of my own. The only thing I knew how to do was the "Square Rig"—slide, step, slide in a square pattern. Two Princeton sophomores were also on hand paying court to Ingrid. They were handsome, athletic types who occupied all her time, while I raked and rolled the tennis court and avoided the icy swimming pool and the dance floor. Even twelve-year old Marianne paid me little attention, as she was entertaining visiting girlfriends. They seemed to spend a great deal of time lurking in corners and giggling while they peeked at Ingrid and her swains.

My one real ally during that weekend was Adele Rouge, the cook, housekeeper, and veritable manager of the Shellabarger family. Her kitchen was my refuge where I could sample her *chef d'oeuvres* and listen to her commentaries and advice, expressed in a colorful French accent.

I saw Marianne about three years later in 1935. Ingrid had been married the year before at age eighteen to Bill Rea of Pittsburgh. Thus she was safely removed from any romantic liaison with me. However, the two mothers had not given up their plan for a grand alliance between the Shellabargers and Jeppsons. Marianne and I were still single. Without consulting me, my mother invited Marianne to be my partner at Worcester's Bachelors Ball, an annual dinner dance held at the Tatnuck Country Club in December. It was a costume party. The bachelors brought their own ladies, who were usually the current debutantes. At fifteen, Marianne would have been considered too young for the ball, but Mother felt that since no one in Worcester knew this lovely Princeton, New Jersey girl, she would pass muster. To make doubly sure, she gave Marianne a sophisticated, upswept hair-do and dressed her in a French gown that Father had brought back from Paris. Finally, she made up Marianne's face to look a few years older and embellished her with fine jewelry.

I dressed up as Eugene Sandow, one of the world's strongest men— well known in the early 1900s. He was a vaudeville star of note and had written books about how to build the body beautiful, which I, of course, had studied. As a costume, I wore long white underwear, a fancy red cape, a wide silk sash, and a black beard and moustache. Cotton was stuffed inside my underclothing to enhance my biceps, thighs, and calves. During the evening, no one could guess whom I was portraying. Eventually, my slim figure won out in spite of my efforts to enlarge it. The cotton stuffing would not stay put. I looked more lumpy than muscled, and there were those who thought I had some dreadful disease. The majority guessed I had come as Rasputin, the Russian villain.

Without question, Marianne was the belle of the ball and danced with all the men to the music of Lester Lanin and his band. Ballroom dancing was in vogue—fox trots, waltzes, tangos, rumbas, and polkas. Partners danced face-to-face, the man holding his partner's right hand with his left. His right arm and hand were around her lower back, as she placed her left hand on her partner's shoulder. There were many variations to the dances. Partners could hold each other closely or not. They could dance cheek-to-cheek. Twirls and dips were accomplished by good dancers. Yet despite these changes and additions, each dance had its basic form. Dances were formal yet exciting. The room full of young men and beautiful girls moving gracefully in cadence to good music was a sight never to be forgotten.

The ball lasted until 2:00 a.m. The Bachelors could not afford to extend Lester Lanin's contract. Marianne and I drove back to my house at 1 Drury Lane, but that didn't end our adventure. Still full of vim and vigor, we put on boots and hiked through snow up the steep hill to Bancroft Tower. We mounted the stone stairs to the top, where we could see all of the city of Worcester and its environs. The moon shone, as did the stars. It was the perfect setting for love to bloom. It did not. Marianne was too young and I was too shy. We never got beyond holding hands.

In February of 1937, I represented Amherst College at the Millrose Games in Madison Square Garden in New York City. I was a member of the mile relay team and was also invited to run the high hurdles at that annual international track meet. Mother called me a few days before it took place and said, "John, when you are in New York you must look up Marianne Shellabarger. She has just graduated from Edgewood School and is temporarily staying with her sister, Ingrid, before entering the University of Florence in Italy." Neither Marianne nor I was very excited by the thought of another meeting. But we dutifully met at Madison Square Garden where I had purchased a couple of seats for the two of us and where she could see me in action in my events. My performance was not too bad—a win with our relay team and place in the final heat of the hurdles. Marianne seemed impressed and agreed to have a late supper with me at Jack Dempsey's that evening. As I saw her walk into the restaurant after the meet was over, I realized that I was dating a beautiful girl—face, figure, posture, graceful walk, and lovely contralto voice. It was again a time for love to bloom, but again it did not. As our first course was served, I tipped the scrambled eggs into my lap, and had to be mopped up by an irritated waiter. By the time this mishap was taken care of, it was time for Marianne to take the train to Riverdale where her sister lived and time for me to return to Amherst. She took the steamer to Italy the very next day. I sent red roses to the boat and included a card with the stirring phrase, "love from John." Marianne did not know which of her many suitors named John had sent the roses. Consequently, I never heard from her. In fact, we did not meet again for nine years.

Life took us both in different directions during this long span of time. While attending the University of Florence, Marianne joined a dance company to learn classical ballet, which took her to Lake Lugano, Switzerland for the summer months. It was her intention to continue her art history courses for another year, but the signing of the Munich Pact, giving in to Hitler's demands, meant to some that war was on the horizon. Foreigners were urged to return home. Marianne left her beloved Italy and, for the first time in her life, was at loose ends. So she decided to attend Katherine Gibbs Secretarial School in New York City. On graduating, she spent the summer in Wiscasset, Maine, where she learned to fly a Piper Cub and acquired a private pilot's license. She also became engaged to be married, but broke it off—fortunately for me.

Having had enough leisure and romance, Marianne went to work. Her first job was helping to run debutante parties in New York City for Clementine Miller. The year 1939 was a festive glittering season. Pearl Harbor was in the future, but money was being raised to support Britain's war effort. Subscription dances were held on Britain's behalf. One season was enough for Marianne. She said goodbye to the big city and took a job in Columbus, Ohio, where her family was living at the time. She spent the next two years working for Curtiss-Wright and its chief test pilot, Red Hulse. It was an exciting and worthwhile time, but right after Pearl Harbor, Marianne decided to leave for Washington, D.C., to be nearer the center of things. She was fortunate to get a job with the North American Aviation Office. It turned out to be another stepping stone to service overseas with the American Red Cross.

Washington was an exciting place to be, but still not close enough to the action. Marianne found out about a newly formed branch of the Red Cross that was opening up, an experimental entertainment club on wheels known as Clubmobile. The applicants were thoroughly screened and Marianne had the good fortune to be interviewed by the former athletic director of the Columbus School for Girls, where Samuel Shellabarger was the headmaster. Her fluency in French and Italian, early recruitment, and a little pull got Marianne over to the British Isles in the beginning of January 1943.

Her job was to serve coffee and doughnuts, play music and provide good cheer to thousands of young men, many of whom had never been far from home. They were a mobile club, seen today and gone tomorrow, bringing a touch of home to homesick boys. The Clubmobiles were assigned to various army units soon after D-Day. Marianne's Clubmobile followed Patton's Third Army to Czechoslovakia. She and her "comrade in arms," Charlotte Colburn, were never far from the front lines. Seeing two such attractive girls offering music, coffee and

*Marianne waving from the back
of a Red Cross Clubmobile truck (1942)*

doughnuts—and good cheer—did wonders for the morale of the battle weary troops. General Patton personally expressed his gratitude for what the Clubmobile girls accomplished.

The end of the war brought Marianne home to Columbus where she helped her father research and type his second, successful, historical novel, *Prince of Foxes,* released in 1947. This followed *Captain from Castile,* which was on the *New York Times* Best Seller List in 1945.

My nine years *sans* Marianne were also busy and challenging. I finished my formal education at Amherst College in 1938, and Harvard Business School in 1940. I was married to my first wife, Julie, in 1939 and fathered John III in 1941, and Muffy in 1943. I went to work for the Norton Company in 1940. Less than a year later, the company loaned me to the Office of Production Management, which was the predecessor of the War Production Board. Here I joined a group charged with expanding the U.S. production of machine tools needed to supply the thousands of tanks, planes, ships, and guns necessary to win the war.

When the war officially began on December 8, 1941, I immediately volunteered for the U.S. Navy. I was accepted as an ensign in February, and ordered to the Naval Gun Factory in Maryland where I became an expert on all types of naval guns—most of which became obsolete soon after the war began. I was then made a member of the Army-Navy Munitions Board, working again on machine tool production. Tagged as a Harvard Business School graduate, I was given only administrative assignments in the beginning. My constant requests for sea duty only got me as far as gunnery officer of the Northern Sea Lane Patrol, in charge of protecting the East Coast from the Maritimes in Canada to New York City. If Germany and Hitler had known that the only

John Jeppson on VJ-Day (1945)

protection the U.S. had along its East Coast were yachts and fishing boats armed with depth charges and obsolete weaponry, we might have suffered severe attacks on a number of coastal locations. The picture changed quickly when the whole country got behind the war effort.

My final post was as assistant to the captain of the naval ammunition depot in Hawaii. There were six thousand naval officers and personnel stationed there to supply the entire Pacific Fleet with everything from pistol bullets to sixteen-inch guns on battleships, to torpedoes on submarines, and bombs on planes.

When the war was over on VJ-Day in 1945, my first marriage was over too. I returned to the Norton Company. After several months, I was ready for rest and recreation. I had planned a ten-day vacation with my mother and father at their winter home in Palm Beach, Florida.

Matchmaking mothers, Vifvan Shellabarger and Selma Jeppson (1954)

My Navy duty in World War II had ended only a few months earlier, and I had returned immediately to my job at the Norton Company in Worcester. I had not had a real reunion with my parents for several years. A couple of days before I was to fly south, Mother telephoned me. She told me that she had heard from the Shellabargers and that Marianne would be staying with a Red Cross compatriot in Palm Beach during my vacation there. I said, "Oh, Mother! Don't tell me that you and Marianne's mother are still matchmaking? I'm coming to spend time with you and Father and no one else." My protestations went unheeded. My plane arrived in Palm Beach at 1:00 p.m. and a reluctant Marianne and her friend, Mariann Foskett, arrived for drinks at 6:00.

When these two walked into the house and I saw Marianne, amazing things happened to me. Clichés abounded. Angelic music sounded in my ears. A strange and lovely light surrounded Marianne. I could immediately see myself dressed in shining armor, carrying her off to my castle. Marianne experienced none of these same sounds and visions. I was aware that I had just six days to convince her that I was the man of her dreams—only six days remained of her holiday.

Fortunately, Mariann Foskett and Marianne invited me to all the functions that they were attending. The older Fosketts stood well in the community—she, a leading socialite and a volunteer of note; he, a distinguished lawyer known for his handling of Sir Harry Oakes' massive estate in 1943. Oakes was the Canadian mine owner who had been murdered at his Nassau house. The crime was never solved.

Because the war had just ended, this was a time of celebration. For the first time in years, people celebrated without restraint. They let their hair down. They spent lots of money. Rationing was over. The troops were back. Palm Beach was one of the party capitals of the United States. We went to luncheons, pool parties, cocktail parties, dinners and dances. There was even a deep-sea fishing party. It was hard to see Marianne alone during all this social activity, but I always managed to be in close attendance.

One luncheon deserves special mention. It was at the Seeburgs. He was the inventor of the Seeburg Nickelodeon, an automatic record player, which, in those days, we could see and hear in nearly every drug store, soda fountain, bar, or roadside restaurant. They were closed machines with impressive chestnut-veneered cabinets with a glass opening through which we could see the records being played and changed. A coin slot on the side took the money—five cents per record. At the Seeburgs' palatial home, we sat in our bathing suits at tables shaded by large beach umbrellas. At their enormous pool, attendants pushed cock-tails out to the swimmers on floating trays.

During the last two days of Marianne's stay in Palm Beach, I was able to corral her after the day's events were over. We found a very pleasant little restaurant and bar, the Pelican Club, where we conversed in reasonable privacy. We found that we had common views on a great many things and that we enjoyed each other's company. We even held hands as we talked and, when the Pelican closed, I walked her home and kissed her goodnight. We met again at the club the next evening, where everything happened very much like the night before. It was her last night in Florida and, at the end of the evening, we began to walk back to our respective places. Here fate stepped in. One of us, or perhaps the two of us at the same moment, said, "Let's go back by way of the beach." We took off our shoes and stockings and walked barefoot in the soft sand. The moon was nearly full, and there was a gentle tropical breeze. The noise of the surf was just enough to muffle other sounds. I will say no more, except that this was when we plighted our troth and a shooting star sealed the bargain.

The following morning at breakfast, I told my parents that I was going to marry Marianne. They were overjoyed. I told them that I was going out that morning to buy her a piece of jewelry to make her think of me when she wore it at the Mardi Gras in New Orleans—her next stop. Father said, "John, I'm coming with you to be sure you buy some-thing good enough for Marianne." Sixty years later, she still wears the golden horseshoe with its seven red rubies. It has brought us both more good luck than we deserve.

Though her trip to New Orleans was to be the first Mardi Gras after the conclusion of World War II, and though she was sought after by many young "lotharios," she remained true to me upon her return to her family in Columbus, Ohio. Marianne thought, as I did, that the next step in our relationship was for me to visit her family and get their blessing.

My trip to Columbus was not the best. Bad weather diverted my flight to Detroit, where I spent the night sitting up in an airport waiting room too crowded to lie down in. Things cleared up the next morning, and I was able to get an early flight to Columbus. I took a taxi to the Shellabargers' house. While I was walking up their driveway, a window opened in the house next door. A feminine head popped out and shouted, "John Jeppson, what are you doing out here in Columbus?"

I said, "I'm visiting the Shellabargers."

The congenial face in the window was that of Vera McElroy, formerly Vera Bullock of Worcester, with whom I had attended the Bancroft School. She was a longtime friend. I also knew her as a very good communicator and that she would put two and two together. I knew that my intentions toward Marianne would be known by a fair slice of my hometown friends by eventide.

I got to the door and was greeted by the Shellabargers' remarkable *major-domo*, Adele Rouge. She took one look at my unshaven face and wrinkled clothing and ushered me into a bathroom. She took my coat and trousers away to iron them and by the time I had shorn the whiskers off, the clothes were returned. Adele was really rooting for me and didn't want my bedraggled appearance to affect the Shellabargers' assessment of me as a future son-in-law. I was now ready for anything and could not wait to see my Marianne. I had arrived before breakfast and greeted the family as they descended the stairs. Marianne's mother led the procession—good looking, tall, erect. She had represented her native Sweden as an Olympic gymnast in the 1912 games in Stockholm. Marianne's father came next, looking every inch the erudite headmaster and professor. Buoyed by the success of his recent best seller, *Captain from Castile*, he projected an aura of good feeling. Last down the stairs came Marianne. I swept her into my arms.

After a large breakfast, Marianne's father ushered me into his library. He sat me in a comfortable chair, offered me a cigarette, and we had a very relaxed talk together. But it was also serious. We discussed my divorce and my two children as well as my prospects and what I hoped to accomplish in life. He had a facility for getting me to talk about myself. We wound things up talking about our religious beliefs. What we discussed in that library that day in 1946 might seem archaic in today's world, but out of it came a great respect for Marianne's father and his family. It was the beginning of a warm friendship.

Next, Marianne visited *Oakholm* to meet my two children for the first time: John and Julie—better known as Jonathan and Muffy. They were then five and four years old, and Marianne was concerned about how things would turn out. Would they resent her? Would they feel that she was trying to usurp the position of their mother? Her fears turned out to be groundless, mainly because she handled the situation with intelligence and good sense. She made no effort to take their mother's place. She did not smother them with questions. In a quiet way, she learned about their interests, their likes and dislikes. She posed as a friend, and not a surrogate mother. Many years later, the warm friendship that she has developed with them is stronger than ever. She has their respect and vice versa. She has been the referee that they could go to when their mother and I disagreed on matters affecting them. They have also become close to Eric and Ingrid, the children Marianne and I had together.

Our next meeting was in early June of 1946, the day before Marianne and her mother sailed to Sweden to visit friends and relations and to attend a PEN club conference in place of Samuel Shellabarger, who was unable to attend. It seems that ever since we met as children at *Oakholm*, she was always leaving me for some place more interesting and more glamorous. Several times her trips deferred any possibility for our love to bloom. But the trip to Sweden was different. We had weathered New York, Palm Beach, New Orleans, Columbus and *Oakholm*. Our families were fully behind us. A few weeks apart would have no effect on anything, but our patience was wearing thin.

In Sweden, Marianne bought a sofa, chairs, and tables for our future home, reinforcing the fact that our marriage was destined to take place. This reduced my anxiety when I received her letters describing parties and dances with handsome young men in attendance.

Our wedding date was finally set for January 15, 1947, a year after we had become engaged in Palm Beach. The place for the ceremony was to be Trinity Episcopal Church in Princeton, New Jersey. The Shellabargers had moved back to Princeton from Columbus when Marianne's father's success with his novels enabled him to resign from the Columbus School for Girls, and write full time. Princeton had been the Shellabarger's home base for most of their lives, and they were more than happy to return to it.

Immediately, there was a hitch in their plans for Marianne's and my wedding. The local minister refused to marry us because I had been

Marianne and her parents, Samuel and Vifvan Shellabarger,
and Adele Rouge (1947)

divorced, even though the divorce involved no fault on the part of me or my former wife. Marianne's family was furious. Her father was a devout Episcopalian. He discussed the situation with his close friend, Bishop Donald B. Aldrich, who pointed out that it was Episcopal church law to refuse to marry a couple where one or both of the celebrants had been divorced and that he could do nothing about it. A still furious Samuel Shellabarger gave me the bad news. My Lutheran church had no such regulations against our marriage, and I was delighted to report to Marianne and her family that my minister, Victor Beck, would be happy to tie our knot in Princeton on January 15 at their lovely home on Library Place.

On January 14, Mother, Father, and family drove to New York to stay overnight at the Waldorf Astoria Hotel. I did likewise, driving Pastor Beck. It was our plan to do the hour's drive to Princeton the following morning, allowing plenty of time to reach the Shellabargers' home prior to the noon wedding ceremony.

The great day arrived. My family left for Princeton at 10:00 a.m. The Pastor and I left a half hour later. A freezing rain began just after we crossed the Hudson River to the Jersey shore. Route 1 was a disaster—solid ice. We proceeded at a slow speed, and after thirty minutes I realized that the groom and his minister would be late for the wedding. Consequently, I put just a little more weight on the accelerator pedal, bringing the speed up to fifty miles per hour. I braked at the next red light, but skidded right through it, missing a large moving van by inches. A few miles farther, my overly zealous braking caused the car to turn full circle. By this time I was sweating and Pastor Beck was praying. I firmly believe that the good Lord listened to his prayers. We drove safely into the Shellabargers' driveway at exactly noon.

We were hastily ushered into the large library room with books from floor to ceiling. At the far end was a great carved stone fireplace and mantle—the place where we were to be married. Everyone was present except the bride. The wedding march from the opera *Lohengrin*—"Here comes the bride"—was being played at the piano with great gusto by John Basore, a close family friend and a professor of Latin and Greek at Princeton University. Still no Marianne. Halfway through the second rendition, Marianne appeared looking just a bit flustered. She had promised herself that she would finish typing the manuscript of her father's newest book, *Prince of Foxes*, the second of his historical novels,

Marianne and John Jeppson (1951)

before marrying me. Our ceremony was, therefore, ten minutes late.

Marianne looked lovely in a beige silk cocktail dress with a Cymbidium orchid corsage. But as Pastor Beck read the beautiful words, his hands holding the Bible were shaking noticeably, a delayed reaction to his wild ride with the groom. On the mantle above us and looking sternly down upon us was a bust of Dante, as if to say "Always be good to each other or you'll hear from me!"

After the vows were exchanged, a lunch was provided by Adele and company. I can't remember what we ate, but the champagne punch was delicious. We had such a good time with family and friends, including several Red Cross girls with whom Marianne had served in Europe, that Marianne's mother had to push us out the door.

Our wedding ends this story, but our romance continues to flourish at *Oakholm* sixty years later.

Part Two

A MAN FOR HIRE

John Jeppson hard at work (2007)

A Man for Hire

WHEN MY MOTHER AND FATHER were living at *Oakholm*, it was operated in a very different manner than it is today. It was a dairy farm and horses were used to work the fields. Hay and cattle corn were the important field crops. Vegetable gardens were cultivated with hoes, shovels and rakes. Trees for firewood, fence posts, and lumber were cut with hand axes and hand saws. Logs were split with heavy mauls and wedges. Lawns were cut by manually-pushed machines. *Oakholm* was a much quieter place in the 1920s, 30s and 40s than it is now. The lowing of cattle, the neighing and snorting of horses, the distant barking of dogs, and the singing of birds were the most prevalent sounds. Train whistles were heard a few times a day, and the bell in the town hall told us, country folk, when it was time to eat.

The only noise that was harsher then than now was caused by numerous outboard motor boats used by fishermen and enthusiasts on weekends. The exhaust of outboard motors was vented into the open air, causing a deafening noise. Half a dozen of these motor boats on the lake sounded like an equal number of low-flying fighter planes and could ruin Sunday afternoons for those of us living along the shore. Laws are now in effect requiring underwater exhausts, reducing engine noise.

The preponderance of hand labor on a farm, when my parents first settled into *Oakholm*, required more people. Stellan needed a full-time hired man for operations—milking, caring for cattle, haying, wood-cutting, and driving work horses. During haying and harvesting seasons, two or three part-time laborers were added. Mother employed a gardener, with the appropriate name of Bees, to maintain a greenhouse and large vegetable garden and to help with flower and rock gardens. He was very good at his trade, and I can see him now carrying baskets full of vegetables and flowers up to the house.

Jefferies, the dairyman, bottled and then cooled the milk bottles, churned butter, cleaned glass bottles, and delivered milk to wholesale customers. It is remarkable to me that one man could accomplish so much on his own with relatively limited support from others. But that was the ethic back then.

Jones was our horseman for several years. He took care of seven horses—groomed, fed and exercised them when we were away. Keeping the leather saddles, bridles and harnesses in good order came under his purview as did carriages and sleighs. Jones was a bandy-legged little man, an Englishman with a cockney accent that was almost unintelligible. He had served in the British army in the Near East in an area formerly controlled by Great Britain and told exciting tales of his duty there.

On a summer evening in 1930, he saw me bouncing a soccer ball against a barn door and asked me to let him have it for a few minutes, whereupon he demonstrated a series of amazing moves and tricks. It turned out that he had been a forward on a championship, regimental team in Syria. He took me in hand and spent the rest of the summer teaching me how to play soccer well—so well that I captained varsity teams at Deerfield Academy and Amherst College.

Clarence Crooks, the family chauffeur, drove Mother when she shopped, drove Father when cataracts dimmed his eyesight and did a myriad of other odd jobs for them. Mother's staff, the aforementioned Three Graces, ran the household under her auspices.

Oakholm is operated in a radically different way these days. A few cattle are raised for beef, and we have a small flock of turkeys. There is no dairy. The haying is totally mechanized. With the right equipment, it can be handled by one or two men. Field corn is no longer raised. Vegetable gardens are very small. Forests are managed and selectively cut by outside contractors. We lease some of the hay fields. We raise Christmas trees and sell raspberries and blueberries.

Marianne takes care of everything involving the large main house, including the fixing of gourmet meals. She employs one person to help clean the house four hours per week. An apartment over the garage, called the "Casita" and the family club, the *J House*, are under her wing as well. My duties involve gardens, pruning, brush cutting and various caretaking assignments, with Paul, our farmer, doing everything else.

Mother and Father employed eight full-time staff at *Oakholm* with additions at hay and harvest seasons. Marianne and I employ one man full-time and part-time people thirteen hours per week. How and what we farm requires less labor, and converting hand operations to machines has reduced labor as well. However, the major difference between then and now is the change in our lifestyle. Informality reigns at *Oakholm*. We have no household staff. We employ no gardener and no chauffeur. Marianne, Paul Benjamin, and I do it all, yet *Oakholm's* buildings, gardens, fields and forests look just as well as they ever have. We have often said to each other that we could make lots of money as a "hired couple" working for one of the billionaire Baby Boomers. Sometimes we think we might prefer it.

High Flyers

ONE EVENING IN THE summer of 1948, Father said to Mother, "The Sofia girls will be here in July. What shall we do for them?"

"Why do we have to do anything?," Mother said, "They're on tour and will be too busy to be entertained by us in any way."

Marianne and I were visiting at the time. We admitted to knowing nothing about the Sofia girls. We learned that they were from Sweden and world-renowned gymnasts. Their director, Maja Carlquist, had developed rhythmic, acrobatic, flowing dance performances using no equipment except a few large balls and jump ropes. She usually traveled with a troupe of about fifteen young women, all about the same size and build. They performed barefoot. All wore the same light blue uniform—sleeveless, with rounded necklines and short-skirts that flowed slightly during the movements of the dance. Carlquist derived her costume design and many of the movements of her dances from athletes as depicted by great ancient Greek sculptors such as Praxiteles, Lysippus and Myron of Eleutherae—for example, Zeus about to throw a spear, Hermes running and the Discus Thrower.

As he was usually able to do, Father convinced us that we should invite Maja and her troupe to spend an afternoon and evening at *Oakholm* on the day following their performance in Worcester. It would give them a chance to rest up after a multitude of performances around the United States.

Soon after this conversation, I was approached by a Worcester contingent about hosting the members of the Swedish soccer team, Djurgården A.C., who were then European champions. They were also on an American tour and were scheduled to play teams from various cities and states. Soccer was then—as it still is today—the major world sport, but was not nearly as popular in the U.S. as it is now. It was a rapidly growing sport, however, particularly in private schools and colleges. I had played for Deerfield Academy and Amherst. Also, there were local teams, composed usually of immigrants from European, African, and South American countries. Two teams of Swedes had been organized in Worcester, the Swedish American and the Scandinavian Athletic clubs. Besides Swedes, there was a sprinkling of Scottish, Irish and English on these teams.

The only date available for the Swedish soccer champions to play in Worcester was the same day that the Sofia Girls were to perform. We told Mother and Father that we could take on the soccer team, leaving them to entertain the Sofia Girls. Father said, "Nothing doing. We'll invite the soccer team out to *Oakholm* along with the Sofia Girls. There will be about the same number of young men and women and it will be a good party." And it was. They got along famously and we are certain that several romances had their origin at *Oakholm* on the shores of Lake Quaboag. The Sofia Girls graced us with an impromptu performance with the lake as backdrop. The weather was perfect, as it always seemed to be when Mother and Father held a party.

There is a sequel to the visit of the Swedish soccer team to Worcester that had beaten the New England All Stars easily, with a final score of ten to three. The outstanding player on the team was the center forward, Hans Jeppson. Though his last name was spelled exactly like ours, sadly we could find no blood relationship between us. Within a few years he became Europe's leading professional player, which made him the highest paid as well. Like Babe Ruth and Joe DiMaggio in baseball, he became an icon in his sport—known everywhere.

In 1954 about six years after the picnic with the soccer team and dancers at *Oakholm*, business called me to Europe. Marianne was with me when the European part of my trip ended in Rome. We were about to take off by air for Johannesburg, South Africa, and as we walked over the tarmac to board the plane, a crowd of photographers and newspaper reporters surrounded us. This was a time when the press was allowed on airfields in Italy. Also, it was a time when one walked from the waiting room to the spot where the plane was parked and climbed the steps to enter the plane. At that time, planes were mainly propeller driven. Ours was a DC4. Photographers took pictures of us every step of the way and, not until we were safely ensconced in our seats, did we learn why we had so suddenly become famous. The day before, Hans Jeppson, the international soccer star, had married an Italian princess with great pomp and ceremony. He was then playing with the Milan team, number one in Europe, and was known and admired by everyone. Although the wedding was well publicized, the honeymoon had been kept a complete secret. The press had been checking all airlines, as well as every other means of travel, and came across the names of a couple named "Jeppson" embarking for South Africa. Hence our adventure at Rome's airport.

OUR GUESTS HERE TODAY — WE CORDIALLY WELCOME THEM TO OUR CITY

World-renowned Swedish soccer team and Sofia Girls visit Worcester (1948)
From the *Worcester Telegram*

Marianne and I were quite proud of being taken for the beautiful princess and Hans Jeppson, the handsome athlete.

When we were settled in our seats with buckled seat belts, a distinguished gentleman across the aisle tapped me on the shoulder and said, "I'm delighted to sit across the aisle from you and your wife, but apologize for not knowing who you are." It was Thomas J. Watson, Jr., president of I.B.M.

The Flood of 1954-1955

THE HURRICANE OF 1938 remains the most powerful storm to hit *Oakholm* during the family's eighty-year ownership of the property. But the storm that swept through Central Massachusetts in 1954 dropped over eighteen inches of rain in thirty-six hours, two inches more than the hurricane of 1938. The fields and forests surrounding Lake Quaboag were swamped when the three dams designed to control overflow from the old North Brookfield reservoir, Brooks Pond and Lake Lashaway, washed out. When these dams were rebuilt after the 1938 hurricane, the Army Corps of Engineers had assured us that we would never be flooded again. The new dams would never fail. But fail they did, and we were once more awash in floodwater. Once again the *J House*, our clubhouse by the lake, was flooded to the eaves and once again the chimney and fireplace anchored it, preventing it from floating away.

In 1954 when the storm hit, Marianne and I were living at *Timberock*, a house near *Oakholm* that had been given to us by Mother and Father. As children, we called it the "haunted house." Vacant for years, it was windowless and battered, with no siding or plumbing, and without a roof. But its frame was in good shape and it was located on a knoll seventy feet above the lake. The setting was beautiful.

137

Timberock, *". . . so ugly that it's beautiful."* *(1955)*

We restored the house in 1949, and loved our summers there until we moved over to the main house at *Oakholm* in 1976. The house was built on a rock ledge, and looked like a two-story Swiss chalet on the side facing the lake and like a Worcester three-decker apartment house from the back. The windows in the back were installed off-center in order to accommodate the rear stairway. Our good friend, Jens Frederick Larson—the architect of the Baker Library at Dartmouth and buildings at Colby College and Wake Forest University—looked at it carefully and concluded, "That house is so ugly that it's beautiful."

When the 1954 flood waters surrounded *Timberock*, our knoll became an island. The house and garage were well above flood level,

John Jeppson and son Eric navigating the flood waters (1955)

but much of the long road leading to them was covered by six feet of water. When this occurred, I was at my office at Norton Company in Worcester. Marianne called to give me the bad news that *Timberock* was inaccessible by car.

We agreed to a plan. I would drive as far as I could down our long entrance road and honk my horn three times when I could go no farther. This would be a signal for Marianne to paddle down the flooded road in our Old Town canoe to pick me up. When it was time for me to go to work the next day, she would paddle me to the car.

Our plan worked perfectly, but we had to be careful to avoid touching power lines which were hanging only three or four feet above the water. (The sight of lovely Maid Marianne paddling through the Sherwood Forest to meet her Robin Hood is one I still treasure.) A reassuring picture greeted us as we arrived at the end of the road. Nanny and Hugo Carlson—a couple employed by and living with us—were preparing a sumptuous meal over a charcoal grille on our "island." The family was together and, although we had no power for five days, we gorged ourselves on everything in our freezer before it had a chance to spoil.

The next morning, Hugo and I took four-year old Eric, seated between us in the canoe and fitted with an orange-colored "Mae West," and paddled around the flooded areas to assess the damage. Just south of *Timberock*, we had built a three-rail fence around a two-acre field that served as our summer horse pasture. The field was totally covered by water and the buoyancy of the rails had pulled the fence posts out of the ground—even though they had been set three feet below ground level. Most of the fence had come apart and hundreds of rails and posts were scattered over the surface of the water. In and around the floating fence parts were gas tanks for cooking and all sorts of other debris that had made its way onto our submerged property from summer camps across the lake.

I took to saying, "Uh-oh," every time I saw a new problem—a flooded house, a loose boat, an errant wharf, a floating lawn chair. After commenting in this manner for the umpteenth time, Eric anxiously complained in his four-year old, flutelike voice, "Don't say 'uh-oh' all the time, Daddy!"

It took about ten days for the floodwaters to recede and another month to complete the cleanup. Ultimately, the dams holding back the waters above Lake Quaboag were rebuilt and once again the Army Corps of Engineers assured us that they would never wash out.

Thundering Hooves

DURING ITS HEYDAY as a farm, *Oakholm* had a fine herd of Guernsey cattle producing milk in substantial volume that was sold at prices substantially below cost. In addition to losing money, there were aggravations such as resolving prickly personnel issues, filling out complicated government forms and paying frequent bills. These made weekends less than relaxing, especially after working hard at the Norton Company during the rest of the week. In 1980, we sold the cattle and some of our acreage, vowing to simplify life at *Oakholm*. We wanted to make it a place of serenity and peace—a place where one could commune with nature and commune only once in a while with people.

We sold cattle, yes, but what we had left included all the buildings: four houses, four barns, and at least ten out-buildings, such as dairies, manure pits, chicken house, carriage shed, tool shed, and boat house. Most of the buildings were under-utilized but attractive and Marianne and I, being stubborn people, wanted them to stay that way. Marianne now slaves inside while I slave outside, trying to do what chauffeurs, gardeners, cooks, maids, farmers and hired men used to do.

Although *Oakholm* was no longer a commercial farm, we felt it ought to have the appearance and feel of a farm so that our family—especially our grandchildren, and great-grandchildren—would learn to appreciate the land. We wanted them to understand that it produces the most basic and important products of our country. In order to re-create the ambience of a working farm, including the aromas, we decided to bring back a few farm animals, restore the hay fields, and continue to maintain the gardens.

We mastered the gardens and the fields, but were ultimately trumped by the animals—especially the draft horses. It all started with one pair that we used for pulling old sleighs, wagons, and equipment to show friends and family how farming was done in yesteryear. We soon began to hear about the growing demand for these animals. More and more people were raising them for show purposes, for forestry work, and for use on small farms. In an attempt to reduce pollution, Japan entered the market buying stallions and mares for breeding. They hoped to replace tractors on small farms. Having an unused barn and sufficient land for pasture and hay, we decided to buy and breed a few Belgians.

We chose Belgian horses rather than Percherons, Clydesdales or Haflingers for several reasons. They are the most popular workhorse breed which makes buying and selling easier. They are also the heaviest, strongest, and gentlest of all breeds. And they have a compelling history.

Fairly new to this country, the first having been imported in 1866, their lineage can be traced to the strong Flemish horses already well-known when Caesar conquered Gaul two thousand years ago. They hauled wagons for the Roman armies and were the chargers ridden by Medieval knights in full armor. In all endeavors, Belgians made their presence well known. In my experience, the expression "thundering hooves" had seemed hyperbolic when referring to horses. I was used to the clippety-clop of a saddle horse on pavement or the turf-cutting rustle of race horses on a track. At *Oakholm,* "thundering hooves" took on fresh meaning the first time we heard a few two-thousand pound animals gallop across our pasture. The ground literally shook. Imagine, if you will, an ancient battle with hundreds of these beasts racing on a collision course.

A few facts about Belgian horses. The average weight of an adult is 1,800 to 2,200 pounds. Height is roughly six feet at the shoulder. A full-grown animal can pull three to five tons on a wagon ten hours a day. It will eat three hundred bales of hay per year and twelve quarts of grain per day and produce six tons of rich, brown, aromatic fertilizer annually. Their productive life is generally from eighteen months to twenty years of age.

In order to make our horse-breeding venture more than a twinkle in the twilight of our years, we offered partnerships to the next generation in the family. It took some cajoling and a few threats but we succeeded in persuading our children and their spouses into joining the venture.

We began by purchasing two registered, five-month old fillies from a farm in Vermont. The farm itself was not particularly impressive. We had to thread our way through cats, dogs, chickens, sheep, and a pig or two just to get to the owner's front doorstep. On the other hand, the horses, when we finally located them in a distant pasture, were superb. There were thirty in all, plus two handsome imported sires with impeccable lineage.

We were off to a good start, but there was one disadvantage to buying such young horses—we could not breed them until they were at least two and a half, and it would take another eleven months of gestation for a foal to arrive. It would be a long and sad three years before we would hear the patter of tiny hooves at *Oakholm*. We therefore kept our "weather" eyes out for a brood mare or two, and perhaps even a stud.

Marianne and I personally canvassed most of the prospects in New England and New York State but found the pickings slim and the prices high. We began casting our eyes farther west to Ohio, Indiana and Illinois where the majority of these animals are bred and raised. We read up on sales and auctions and learned which breeding farms were considered the best. Finally, we decided to attend an auction in Topeka, Indiana, where several leading candidates were being placed for sale.

In order to buy the right horses, I travelled to Topeka with our farm manager at the time and my son-in-law, Michael Mach. We arrived at Topeka at noon the day before the auction and found the town to be peopled largely by Amish. We had come to the right place. There were more horses and more buggies than automobiles, since most of the local farming—plowing, cultivating, haying—was done by horses, not machines. The Amish kept the Belgians thriving as a working breed despite the fact that tractors and other machinery had long been the rule on nearly all our nation's farms.

We were hungry when we arrived and were directed to an Amish restaurant where we paid three dollars for soup, pork, two vegetables, salad and a monstrous slab of delicious cherry pie served by young ladies dressed in dark blue dresses, white aprons, and bonnets. The men wore blue denim coats and pants and broad-rimmed black hats with low crowns. They all had beards under their chins and, among the more venerable, the beards reached enormous proportions.

The horse auction in Topeka, Indiana (1980)

When we arrived at the auction, the horses were just beginning to be led out of their vans. It was raining and the big Belgians were churning the place into a sea of mud. Nevertheless, over the next six or seven hours we were able to evaluate the animals that interested us and prepare ourselves for the next day's bidding.

We awoke to a sunny, breezy March morning, the great day of the sale. On arriving at the auction grounds, we were greeted by the extraordinary sight of well over one hundred horses and buggies tethered in a single long line. The Amish had arrived *en masse*—two or three hundred strong—to buy, sell, and watch.

The first lots auctioned were new harnesses, wagons, and horse-drawn equipment. We were surprised to discover that the business of making new apparatus of this type was thriving. We had assumed that we would have to collect antiques to properly outfit a draft horse.

At last, the main event began. A young Amish man entered the ring at a run leading the first of what became a parade of three hundred horses. Bringing up the rear was another young man with a whip. Once the auction began, it became clear that we were somewhat out of our league. The auctioneer was completely unintelligible to us, exactly like a tobacco auctioneer. We were a long way from Massachusetts. In fact, we seemed a long way from the 20th century. But we soon managed to get the gist of what was being said. At the end of the day, we wound up as the proud owners of two fine young mares and a proven stallion—all

Mares and foals at Oakholm *(1983)*

three within our budget. They were soon shipped to *Oakholm* where they joined the two Belgian fillies bought in Vermont to form the nucleus of our breeding stock.

Our horses became a magnet to the other workhorse owners and drivers in the area. On weekends, the barn was usually the scene of a small spirited gathering of wiry, weather-beaten individuals discussing the finer points of working breeds. They were especially interested in the relative merits of their horses compared to ours, and regaled each other with exciting equine experiences in a language all their own. Talking was done in a "hunkered down" position, and was punctuated by an occasional well-directed expectoration, or a raucous cackle of laughter.

Three of the regulars were particularly renowned. John Buzzel had been the chief driver during the Bicentennial reenactment of General Knox's epoch artillery march from Fort Ticonderoga to Boston in the winter of 1775. Knox's great feat forced the unprepared British to evacuate Boston. Ken Lane was another memorable regular. He still used his team on real commercial projects—hauling hay and logs in Brookfield. There was also a knowledgeable fellow named Moulton from Holden, whose horses participated in every parade in the area.

We decided to close our Belgian horse business in 1990. The market for these animals had become saturated and prices had dropped substantially. The Japanese had completed their buying program. Though exceptionally gentle, Belgians are giants who seem to break anything they lean against. We were constantly replacing damaged fences, gates, and stalls. But we may have been premature. As gasoline prices rise and alternate sources of energy fail to materialize, draft horses may once again become a cheap source of locomotion and major producers of organic fertilizer. If cars gradually become extinct like dinosaurs and we are confined forever to our front porches and back stoops, we may yet see draft horse breeders tearing through the countryside behind thundering Belgians. Perhaps, they will occasionally sell a young animal at three times the price of a Rolls Royce to keep in pin money, and will buy up the big houses which their present owners will no longer be able to afford to heat.

Fourth of July

OAKHOLM WAS A WORKING FARM and its owners were not socialites. My mother and father had relatively few parties, but when they did entertain, they did it well. Much time and thought went into their planning for special occasions. One such affair was the annual family Fourth of July celebration. Father's military background contributed to the style of the event. In addition to having been a bugler at Worcester's Highland Military Academy and a class officer, he had joined the Massachusetts State Militia, which later became National Guard along with the other state militias in 1903. He had been an artillery man and a sharp-shooter. We still proudly display his medals. He kept his old uniforms in good order in spite of the fact that he had out-grown them laterally. He also had been a member of the Worcester Continentals, an outstanding marching unit with smart uniforms, swords, rifles, and a spirited band.

Every so often he enjoyed telling of marching with the Continentals from the Battery to Grant's Tomb on the occasion of its dedication in New York City. It was a distance of six miles and occurred on the hottest day in a decade. Marching in woolen uniforms and tasseled caps on steamy pavement, thirsty members of the Continentals would occasionally drop out for quick drinks in saloons along the parade route and then run forward to catch up with their unit. According to Father, they had visited seven establishments by the time they approached the reviewing stand which was more than five miles from their starting point at the Battery. The Continentals were a sorry lot—sweaty and red-faced, out of step, rifles carried at various angles. Fortunately, they were halted temporarily just before the reviewing stand. They could see, standing at attention, famous generals who had served under Grant in the Civil War and other dignitaries. Joshua Chamberlain, who turned the tide at Gettysburg, was there as was Theodore Roosevelt, then Police Commissioner of New York. Seeing these American icons inspired the disheveled Worcester Continentals. Miraculously, they straightened up and shouldered their guns with precision. The band played *The Battle Hymn of the Republic* perfectly while the soldiers stepped out in unison with eyes turned right as they proudly passed the admiring heroes on the stand. Only one mistake marred the performance of the Continentals on that great day. Noticed by only a few, the fife player was missing. He was found three days later in saloon number six.

At *Oakholm* on the Fourth, Father always began the day by playing *Reveille* on his bugle and firing our saluting canon while Old Glory was being raised on our forty-foot flagpole. By this time the whole household was awake, dressed and ready for the holiday breakfast which consisted of fruit, fried strips of corn meal mush and bacon. The fried corn meal was smothered in maple syrup. During the morning, clusters of small firecrackers were set off, which sounded like machine gun fire. We were given torpedoes, small combinations of pistol caps and black powder. These exploded when thrown at a hard surface like the side of a barn. Later came the Brookfield parade. We were awed by the sight of the town's last Civil War veteran, a still spry ninety-year old, walking with measured step behind the flag bearers.

Most of the afternoon was spent preparing for the evening festivities held at the *J House* located on the shores of Lake Quaboag. Lawns were cut and raked. Tables and chairs were set up outdoors and decorated with red, white and blue flowers and flags. As evening approached, Father fired his canon again and played the mess call on his horn. The clan gathered for the traditional dinner of salmon and fresh peas. It was always touch-and-go whether the peas would be ripe enough by the Fourth and, if so, whether the rabbits and birds would leave us enough to eat. Our family was rather small in the mid-1920s and early 1930s: no grandparents, one uncle, an aunt, two cousins and the five of us. Our farm family, the Petersons, joined us, so we were usually twelve or fourteen at the dinner table. Our meal would end with watermelon for dessert just as darkness fell. Then the most exciting part of the Fourth of July would begin. The children were given sparklers that bristled with streaking flames and made a crackling noise as we ran around. Pinwheels were ignited—wheels of multi-colored fire. These were set on five-foot poles and whirled around, emitting showers of sparks that made a dramatic swishing sound. Next came the Roman candles which shot single stars into the night air. Finally, the great moment arrived when the large rockets were fired from the field next to the *J House*. These were shot towards the lake using a six-foot contraption made with two boards nailed together at right angles, properly braced and slanted towards the lake. One by one, the rockets were fired, arching over the water about a hundred and fifty feet high and, as they reached their zenith, bursting into multiple colors. We were utterly entranced and shouted enthusiastically as Father and Stellan Peterson fired each rocket into the sky. We were even more thrilled when an occasional rocket went off course and threatened the family. People living on other quadrants of the lake fired similar rockets which added to the excitement and beauty of the celebration.

Fireworks at *Oakholm*—even sparklers and firecrackers—are now forbidden by law unless produced and fired by licensed professionals. *Oakholm* celebrations have become totally different. Father and Mother and Britta are no longer with us, but my sister Betty now has an extended family of fifteen and Marianne and I, including ourselves, have four generations that total twenty-one. Adding a few close friends brings the attendance at *Oakholm's* Fourth of July to slightly more than fifty every year. Mother Nature has been good to us, providing sunny weather for thirty years with one exception when it rained so hard that we moved into the main house. There we set up eighty feet of tables—one against the other—from the south to the north end of the house, so we had plenty of room for food and sixty people. Our renditions of patriotic songs never sounded as spirited.

There were other times when predictions of bad weather caused us to temporarily bring electricity into the boat house with extension cords and to set up tables which were never used. The tradition of using the *J House* location is now so entrenched that the family would probably rather stand in pouring rain than be anywhere else on the Fourth—no one even wants a tent. It would destroy the setting.

As it was in Mother's and Father's time, great preparations are made in the immediate environs of the *J House*. Tables are set under

John Jeppson and his four children on the second round of aquavit (2006)
From left, *John III, Ingrid, John, Muffy, and Eric*

three, one-hundred-foot high white pines which Father and I planted as three-foot saplings seventy-five years ago. Close to the lake and higher than all the surrounding trees, they naturally attract lightning so we have fastened lightning rods to them. Even so, a lightning bolt hit one fifteen years ago. Remarkably, the old tree survived and still provides us with cool shade. The shade under pines seems to be cooler than the shade of deciduous trees such as maples or oaks, and the sound of wind rustling through the needles is like music to Marianne and me.

For many years after my parents passed away, Marianne did most of the planning for the Fourth—food, decorations, table settings, drinks, keeping track of attendees, where to put them up, and on and on. It fell to me to be the brawn in the proceedings—setting up the tables and chairs, putting up flags, bringing drinks to the *J House* and lugging all manner of food stuffs including bags and jars of nuts, pickles, chips, and olives. The most important hors d'oeuvre is the pickled herring, called *sil* by those of us with Swedish blood in our veins. We set a large bowl of this delicacy on a special table, along with special Swedish bread. All this requires countless trips from the main house to the *J House* which I make using an old gas-driven golf cart given to me by Marianne many years ago. I use it mainly for carrying tools, potting soil, plants, fertilizer, water and an occasional passenger to the many gardens at *Oakholm*. Without it, I would be dead from exhaustion.

Marianne's major annoyance in planning the festivities is that she never knows how many people are coming until the party starts. Nor is she ever sure just how long everyone is planning to stay. My exasperation is that I never know when the male members of the family will arrive to help. Be all that as it may, when 1:00 p.m. finally arrives on July Fourth, a motley but appreciative crowd of family and friends arrives and the festivities begin. Children quickly change into bathing gear and make for the pool. Teenagers shoot baskets, play tennis, and throw frisbees. Twenty-somethings play bocce on the lawn, row boats, paddle canoes or watch babies. The aged gossip and drink everything from gingerale to martinis, while finding the coolest places to sit, usually under the pines or in the screened in porch.

In addition to family, there are always several friends who find their way to our celebration. Marcus McCorison, who headed the American Antiquarian Society for many years, arrives with a running commentary on life and a ready wit, which are much appreciated. John Herron,

Faithful guests, John Herron and Marcus McCorison,
at the Fourth of July celebration, Oakholm *(2005)*

the architect, comes with his great family of book publishers, newspaper editors, teachers, and designers, their spouses and grandchildren, adding to the tumult. We, of course, are all luminaries.

On a typical Fourth, I call everyone to attention before we sit down to eat and ask them to gather around me. I am dressed as an ancient Viking with my horned helmet, my multi-colored "tunic," my axe made from the "hip bone of an ass" and, in my right hand, a carved staff. Beside me is Marianne wearing a helmet with two yellow braids spilling forth. I point out that in the year A.D. 1000, Leif Eriksson and his troop were the first Europeans to land in America, long before Columbus and the Pilgrims who were "Johnny-come-latelys" by Scandinavian standards. I then show everyone a stone found in Lake Quaboag that was used by Leif and his crew to sharpen their axes and swords. I am regularly astonished that there are skeptics who doubt the veracity of these facts. The story of Leif Eriksson is a prelude to our Swedish drinking song, which accompanies the swallowing of the contents of one-ounce glasses of *aquavit*, the Scandinavian schnapps. Finally, we seat ourselves around long tables under the great pines and dig into the good food brought to the scene by family and friends. During the course of the meal, patriotic songs are sung—*The Star-Spangled Banner, America the Beautiful, The Battle Hymn of the Republic.* The singing is good—plenty of volume and mostly in tune. The afternoon winds down slowly and, around seven o'clock, no one is left but the family clean-up crew. Their job is so well done that the *J House* and its environs show no trace of the onslaught of the Fourth.

When night falls and only a few members of the family are left to rehash the day's events, we can see fireworks in the distance produced by neighboring towns, and we compare the day's events to those of years past—usually the laughable ones. We remember when son Eric's friend Randy fell across the table as he stood up to sing *The Star-Spangled Banner.* When asked what had happened, Randy said, "My legs were crossed!" At another of our celebrations, we realized that one of our guests had been missing for several hours. As you might guess, she was not very noticeable to begin with, as even her name escapes me. We searched the lake for floating bodies and we yelled and canvassed the woods to no avail. Finally, we found her sound asleep behind a bed of high day lilies only a few feet from the *J House* where fifty of us had been singing and cavorting all afternoon. We reminisced about the time John Herron and his six-year old daughter, Molly, tipped their canoe over in the lake. John explained that he was teaching Molly how to save herself when a canoe rolls over. It seemed strange to us that he chose a moment to teach such an important lesson when he was dressed in a jacket and tie and was wearing dress shoes. His car keys still remain among the mud and weeds on the floor of Lake Quaboag.

Before saying our prayers, we close the evening by drinking a toast to John Adams and Thomas Jefferson. Both led the way in crafting the Declaration of Independence and both died hours apart fifty years later on the Fourth of July in 1826.

The J House, *scene of Fourth of July celebrations, past and present (2007)*

The Story of Squirt

IN THE FALL OF 1994, we bought several sheep. Our plan was to have them graze over some of the rougher and steeper hillside areas of the farm to keep them relatively clear. We also had visions of eating some delicious meat raised on the premises and fed with healthy *Oakholm* vegetation.

We bought four ewes and a ram, all of the Suffolk breed. Suffolks are handsome sheep, standing tall with black legs and black faces and otherwise white bodies. They produce quality wool, and are also very good to eat. A mature ewe will weigh one hundred pounds, a ram one hundred and fifty.

The ewes were open—farmer parlance for not pregnant. Normal mating occurs between late September and late October, with lambing usually taking place four to five months later in February or March. We hoped to delay this process by a couple of months, surmising that it would be much easier to deal with baby sheep in the warmer months of April and May.

Our new sheep did well and seemed to enjoy their new pastures and excellent quarters. The ram was kept separate from the ewes until Thanksgiving, but to promote a keen interest in the opposite sex, he was kept in a neighboring pasture where he could see his future wives. When the great day came, he lived up to all expectations and we were convinced that everything would go as planned with new lambs arriving in late April.

Paul Benjamin, who does almost everything at *Oakholm*, began to notice some physical changes in one of the ewes in December. She was filling out more than the others, and her udder was beginning to form. She was obviously in a family way, having had an illicit affair with some unprincipled ram before we bought her.

At 2:00 a.m. on the stormiest, coldest, windiest, and snowiest night of the winter of 1995—on Groundhog Day to be exact—she gave birth. Paul was in the barn with her, and witnessed the arrival of a tiny, wrinkled, four-pound little guy completely devoid of protective wool. Paul and his wife, Jean, quickly went into action. Jean used her hair dryer to keep him warm. They made an enclosure to protect the newborn lamb from the other sheep, and placed him in a box on a blanket with a heating pad underneath. A lamp was rigged overhead to provide light and further warmth. The lamb was too weak to stand up and suckle from his mother. A baby bottle and nipple were found, and the Benjamins milked the momma and tried to feed her offspring. Again, there was frustration as he was too weak to suck from the nipple on the bottle. What to do? They cleverly found an empty dish-washing soap bottle with a squirting device on its top. They filled it with milk and squirted it into the lamb's forced-open mouth. Their technique worked, which is why we christened him Squirt. He barely survived. Even though he was fed every two hours, it was touch and go for nearly a week.

On the fifth day, Squirt staggered to his feet and began to feed from

The ram who caused Squirt's demise (1995)

his ewe mother. This meant that he had to leave his warm box. Aware that the lamb was still fragile, Jean made a little wool coat with holes for his legs to keep him from freezing.

You may wonder why the Benjamins did not simply bring him into their house where all these ministrations could have been performed more easily. When a lamb is removed from his mother, even for a relatively short spell, she will reject it, and you will be forced to feed and care for it for months. From the moment Squirt could feed on his own, he flourished, quickly gaining weight and muscle power. In fact, he was so well-formed and forced to overcome so many hurdles that we were thinking of raising him as a breeding animal—the future chieftain of our prize flock.

In the meantime, the other ewes produced their lambs as expected in April without any complications. The day finally came in mid-May when the ram was to be introduced into the same pasture as the ewes and lambs. Rams are allowed to be with the flock in spring and summer, as they are not interested in mating until cooler weather begins in late September. Paul opened the gate between the ram and the flock, and disaster quickly struck. The ram made a beeline for Squirt who was grazing innocently at the bottom of the hill. Weighing 140 pounds and running downhill at high speed, the ram slammed into Squirt, hitting him squarely in the head and knocking him down. Squirt never got up. His neck was broken. The big old ram knew instinctively that Squirt was not his progeny, and was therefore a rival to be eliminated.

A sad ending to the story of Squirt, you will say, but not entirely. Paul Benjamin scooped up the freshly-killed, eighty-pound lamb, skinned him, butchered him and put him in the deep freezer. The idea of eating Squirt was, at first, totally repugnant to Marianne and me, and to Paul's family as well. However, time and practicality prevailed. The roasts, the chops—in fact every bit of Squirt was delicious—and we can truly say that he did not die in vain.

REQUISCAT EN PACE, SQUIRT

Paul Benjamin

PAUL BENJAMIN HAS BEEN taking care of *Oakholm* since 1993. Whether it be animal husbandry, pruning Christmas trees or fruit trees, haying, gardening, carpentry, repairing equipment or painting, he can do everything and do it well. He is tall, strong and bearded and moves quickly with his two big Airedales, Winston and Teddy, who are in constant attendance. He is a worthy successor to Stellan Peterson, although in between there were a couple of lesser lights. One of Paul's ancestors was a Native American, and I like to think that this may account in part for his ability to work outdoors in any kind of weather and his deep knowledge of the land.

Paul's wife, Jean, is a renowned practitioner of rug hooking. She holds regular classes in the farmhouse for skilled students, and she travels to all parts of the country to teach Master Classes. Her catalogs of patterns and hand-dyed wools are well known to rug-hooking *aficionados* around the country. Two children complete the family—Jeremiah, a successful computer engineer, and Jasmine, a banker.

Currently, Paul is developing a program to restore our hay fields. They have been leased for quite a few years, and have not been properly maintained and fertilized. The haying has been done too late in the season which has allowed weeds to grow and lessens the quality of the hay. With the help of our neighbor and organic farmer, Mark Ledoux of *Overlook Farm*, our fields are now being plowed, harrowed, and planted with pumpkins and sweet corn prior to rotating them back into high quality hay.

We have high hopes that a combination of forest management, well-chosen field crops, berries, Christmas trees, gardens and turkeys can make a small New England farm—like ours—a viable economic proposition. Paul is a key to our success.

Paul Benjamin (2007)

The Icehouse

IN ADDITION TO THE MAIN residence at *Oakholm*, Mother and Father acquired a farmhouse and several outbuildings when they bought the property. These included a cow barn and a separate barn for draft horses, pigs and sheep as well as a chicken house and wood shed. Because of the harsh New England winters, out buildings were located near the farmhouse to make it easier for the farmer and his family to watch over their animals and to carry wood, cattle feed, and milk cans without being overwhelmed by the elements. Heavy equipment—wagons, sleds, plows, and harrows—was stored outside and was kept well-painted, oiled and greased to prevent rotting and rusting.

The most unique building at *Oakholm* was the icehouse where enough ice was stored to last from one winter to the next. It was a small structure measuring ten-feet wide, twelve-feet long and eleven feet to the ridgepole. The roof was shingled, and the sides were covered with clapboards. The heavy front door was divided into top and bottom halves each of which could be opened separately. When I first arrived at *Oakholm* as a boy of eight, I was immediately attracted to this strange little building and went to take a look inside. I unhooked the upper door, swung it out and was greeted by a batch of cool air, which felt mighty good on that hot day in June. A layer of wet sawdust covered the whole interior. Sweeping a bit of it to one side with my hands, I realized it was covering huge blocks of ice that were stacked up about as high as my eight-year old nose. I could not wait to pull out my sheath knife to chip off a sliver of ice to cool my tongue and mouth. But my anticipation was interrupted when I heard Ruben, the farmer's son, bellow, "Cover that ice and shut the door. You're melting the ice!" Frightened, I immediately shut the door and ran the three hundred yards back to our house to avoid any further scolding—or worse—from Ruben.

After supper that evening I asked Father about the icehouse. I learned that the ice was cut in the middle of winter from Lake Quaboag. It was hauled to the icehouse for use in our iceboxes and to the barn to keep the milk from our cows cool until it was shipped to a dairy for bottling. Father said that only about one-third of the ice cut the previous February had been used, leaving enough to last until the next ice harvest the following winter.

The ice harvest took place in February when the ice had reached a thickness of ten inches and the temperature was twenty-six degrees fahrenheit, cold enough to cut the ice in blocks, but not so cold that the individual blocks would stick to each other. There was minimal snow on the lake, so that sweeping and shoveling a path and cleaning an area of the ice to be cut was easy. Conditions were perfect for cutting the ice and hauling it to the icehouse.

The Percherons, Molly and Bess, were hitched to a big two-horse bobsled and driven onto the ice. The ice-cutting equipment was onboard, as well as Farmer Brown, Ruben and me. First, we swept and shoveled the snow off the surface to be cut. Next a weighted horse drawn contraption called an ice plow, with several rows of sharp teeth on it, was pulled over the area digging furrows six or seven inches deep. After the plow was run one way, it was turned to cut grooves at right angles, creating a checkerboard pattern of ice cakes. A special handsaw was then used to cut the squares into individual blocks of ice. The saw was straight-bladed and huge, nearly five-feet long. It was also menacing. Large, coarse saw teeth ran the length of the blade which was managed using a two-handed handle set crosswise to the saw blade. The freed blocks of ice measured twelve by eighteen by ten inches and weighed about eighty pounds each.

One by one, we slid them over the firm ice to the waiting bobsled. Each cake was pushed up a plank with the help of ice tongs and dropped onto the bobsled. Twenty-four cakes, weighing nearly a ton in total, constituted a load. A pair of Percherons like Molly and Bess could pull more, but hauling over ice and snow and up hills was treacherous. A lighter load was a safer load. In winter, workhorses were shod with special shoes that had four screw-in calks that dug into the ice and prevented slipping. When the loaded bobsled reached the icehouse, the ice was unloaded using the plank and tongs and placed in rows in the icehouse. Large quantities of sawdust were stuffed over, under and around each block, providing the necessary insulation to keep the ice cold for twelve months. Three hundred blocks filled the house, enough to maintain ice in the iceboxes on the farm for a full year.

Harvesting and storing ice came to a halt in 1926 and 1927 when mass production of electric refrigerators and coolers began to replace traditional iceboxes on our country's farms and households. General Electric marketed the first cheap refrigerator—one with a round coil on top—and they were soon followed by Kelvinator and General Motor's Frigidaire. From then on, the lake remained untouched except for skaters and fishermen. Icehouses, like ours at *Oakholm* and the mammoth ones used for public storage, were abandoned. Most were torn down.

At *Oakholm*, the triumph of electrical refrigeration over lake ice coincided with Father's decision to buy a new herd of Guernsey cattle after the original one had contracted tuberculosis and been destroyed. As discussed earlier, the cows arrived with a new bull, the large and menacing "Teddy's Choice of Hillstead." At first we did not know where to house him. Why not the unused icehouse? It was the right size for Teddy and could be reinforced with additional planks. We surrounded the icehouse with a strong fence supported by old telephone poles. This offered our great bull an ideal spot to observe his cows and heifers.

The icehouse served as a bull barn for a number of years, but it became vacant once more when artificial insemination of cows supplanted Teddy and his successors. The semen of the best bulls in the world became available, and could be administered by veterinarians or trained specialists. Farmers no longer had to own—and manage—their own bulls for breeding purposes.

Ever adaptable, the icehouse-turned-bull-barn remained empty for a very short time. In 1948, my parents gave *Timberock* to Marianne and me. This wonderful property neighbored *Oakholm*, and was filled with fields, woodlands and lawns. We intended to use it as a summer camp. We rebuilt the ramshackle house to make it livable, and soon found that we needed a place to keep lawn mowers, garden tools, axes, saws, shovels, a tool bench and a Gravely tractor. The empty bull barn was the perfect answer, and Father was delighted to rid *Oakholm* of a surplus building. We jacked the icehouse up, slid a wide trailer under it and using a tractor pulled it the half-mile to *Timberock*. We sited it at the edge of a low-lying field near the vegetable garden. It served admirably as a toolhouse for several years.

The Gravely two-wheel tractor was my pride and joy. I used it for plowing and cultivating gardens and cutting tall grass and brush. It was a powerful well-built piece of equipment, but the tractor needed a strong hand to pilot it and keep it under control. I can recall two incidents when it nearly did me in. The first involved backing the Gravely over a high dirt step to put it under cover in the tool house. It got stuck. Instead of taking the time to reduce the height of the step with a few shovels full of dirt or using a couple of planks as a ramp, I opened up the throttle full blast. It leapt over the step in reverse carrying me with it, slamming and pinning me into the far wall of the tool house. Painful sprains and a few bruises were the price of my stupidity.

On the other occasion, I accidentally drove the Gravely over a nest of yellow jacket hornets when I was running it with a cutter bar to remove weeds and light brush. A cloud of these fierce insects swarmed all over me. Since I was near the house, I ran through the porch door howling with pain from several stings. Marianne yelled at me to get out of the house. At that moment she was feeding our new baby, Eric. She was rightly far more concerned about her son's well-being than her husband's demise from hornet stings. I turned about, leapt out of the house, ran down the hill and jumped off the dock into the lake. Happily, I neither drowned, nor succumbed to the stings.

The icehouse served as an all-purpose tool and tractor shed until Lake Quaboag flooded in 1954. The structure floated off its stone foundation and was swept about twenty feet away where it came to rest in a cock-eyed state. Undaunted, we righted the building and rolled it to a higher ground nearer the house. We changed its color from white to good old New England barn-red with white trim. It looked so lovely with its new coat of paint and its background of lilacs, birches and white pines that I made it the subject of my first oil painting. On a beautiful summer day, armed with easel, brush and canvas, I painted for hours. I thought that the final result was comparable to a Turner, an Eakins, or a Wyeth, but few agreed. Perhaps, it will take a century or two for my talent to be more fully appreciated. The painting still exists, but it is hidden behind a door at *Timberock*. Impressively, the subject itself also

The icehouse as painted by John Jeppson (1972)

still exists, although its *raison d'être* has once again changed. It is now a family playhouse where daughter Muffy's progeny enjoy themselves playing billiards. Muffy and her husband, Hal, have turned *Timberock* into an imposing, year-round estate with gardens, guesthouses and lovely lawns.

The icehouse-bull-barn-toolhouse-playhouse stands strong amid all this beauty. What will happen to it next? Perhaps it will become an icehouse again when some cataclysmic event occurs and returns us to the more primitive existence of my childhood.

Varmints

As TIME PASSES, *Oakholm* seems to be invaded by more and more varmints—unpleasant little animals whose main diet consists of plants, fruits, and seeds that we humans like to eat as well. There are some that ruin lawns, trees, flower beds, and vegetable gardens. Every time we think we have a particular species under control, it simply outwits us.

Consider chipmunks. These thick, little six-inch animals are tiny, perky and cute—particularly when they sit up straight on a doorstep or a stone wall to nibble an acorn or hazelnut while their little bushy tails are curled up behind them. Little do people realize that chipmunks, during their winter "hibernation," are not hibernating at all. In their underground bunkers, they are plotting war on us humans. Last year, they planned and executed the complete devastation of our blueberry crop. We had developed an effective netting system to keep the birds from eating the berries, but we never suspected that chipmunks would be the beneficiaries. The chipmunks burrowed under the nets, and ate every blueberry on our bushes. They filled their cute cheeks with them, scampered to the top of a stone wall, and devoured the flesh of the blueberries while daintily spitting out the skins. Telltale patches of blueberry skins covered the top of our fieldstone walls.

Chipmunks have devoured close to ninety percent of all the bulbs of an extensive oriental lily collection that was once our pride and joy. Tulip bulbs are especially delectable tidbits for them. Foxes, coyotes, hawks and eagles are their enemies, but the chipmunk population continues to grow apace. The three cats at *Oakholm* occasionally catch one, but have not frightened them away. Nicodema, our house cat, simply watches in amusement as they jump over her tail and pays no attention while they sit on the nearby stone wall. I have had nightmares about a King Kong-sized chipmunk running off with Marianne and carrying her to the top of the barn silo. In other dreams, millions of the critters dig a hole into which the house falls, and disappears. I have even purchased a high

A nefarious chipmunk (2001)
Photo by kbr photos

powered air rifle in order to eliminate a few of them, but they have a self-protective instinct that makes them jump and scurry to safety just as I get them in my gun sight.

ALMOST EVERYONE HAS SEEN a skunk with its white-striped black body and long black-and-white bushy tail. We've all smelled them, too. When threatened, they can project their odiferous, liquid spray as far as twelve feet. Most of us have had dogs foolish enough to try to attack skunks, and they always get sprayed. We have tried every way imaginable to wash the spray off our pets, but nothing really works. Neither perfumes nor soap and water do much good. Tomato juice removes some of it according to some, but it is a singularly unpleasant experience to wash an eighty-pound white standard poodle in a tub filled with tomato juice. Only time successfully eliminates the scent. Skunks eat rodents, insects, birds, and plants. If you find small, shallow, round holes in your lawn, then it is very likely that a skunk has been digging there for juicy grubs.

Not long ago, a skunk fell into a window well which shed light into our cellar. To make itself known, it sprayed a bit of its scent into the well. We could see the animal through the cellar window and thanked our lucky stars that the window was shut. Our challenge was to figure out how we could get it out of the six-foot deep well. One suggestion, which seemed to me the only feasible solution, was to open the window and try to entice the skunk into the house, up the stairs, and out the front door. Marianne looked at me incredulously when I suggested this solution, saying, "John, do you realize what that little animal could do to this house if something goes wrong? We couldn't live in it for weeks!"

We decided to seek outside assistance. We called Richard Potter, a noted naturalist, and described our skunk problem. He probably knew as much about New England birds and animals as any other person alive, and at that time headed the Worcester Natural History Society, now the EcoTarium. He suggested, "Find an old board long enough to reach the bottom of the window well, place it at an angle, and your skunk will climb up it in two shakes of a lamb's tail." We did as he instructed, and, in no time, our skunk climbed up and out, and scurried away. Q.E.D.

THE NORTH AMERICAN RACCOON has a bushy tail and a black furry mask on its face. It has a stout body, short legs, a pointed muzzle and small erect ears. Its length is thirty to thirty-six inches including the ten inch tail, and weighs about twenty pounds. The coarse fur is grey. Raccoons eat almost everything—from all kinds of small animals to a great variety of fruits and vegetables. Their feet resemble small slender human hands. Consequently, they are good climbers and very much at home in trees. In fact, some live in hollow trees. Though they have become comfortable prowling around residential areas, they are not often seen by us as they are nocturnal animals.

Here at *Oakholm* they cause little trouble. Once in a while they open a garbage can or rob a bird's nest of eggs or fledglings. We tolerate these "incidents" because they assist our cats in catching mice and voles. But in the 1980s, a major change occurred in the habits of the raccoons in the vicinity of *Oakholm*. More and more of them were seen in daylight hours. They attacked cats and snarled fearlessly at dogs. They were acting strangely. We heard from the Massachusetts Department of Fisheries and Wildlife that local raccoons were suffering from an epidemic of rabies, and we were warned that dogs and cats might be bitten and infected with the dread disease. Small children were also at considerable risk.

The time for action had arrived. With my trusty .22 caliber Winchester rifle, I was ready to shoot any rabid raccoon that showed itself in daylight. I fired away at them, but never came close. One fine day, Marianne caught me blearily pointing the gun at our cat as she rounded the corner of the house. After that, my gun was relegated to a locked closet. I thought my high-powered air rifle would be a safe alternative, but cat and dog owners in the family vetoed that as well. So I was forced to come up with another plan.

I purchased a "Have a Heart" trap designed for raccoons and other small animals. The trap consisted of a rectangular steel frame covered by strong, steel netting. Doors at each end slammed down if an animal disturbed a small bait platform located in the center of the trap. Our bait consisted of peanut butter mixed with unsalted pecans. Marianne grudgingly bought pecans annually from her Smith College friends who sold them to raise funds for their alma mater, and we had a large supply of them. This system worked. On the first day a large raccoon was caught. It was daylight, and the furious snapping and snarling of the animal indicated that it was very likely rabid. I picked up the trap with a boat hook to avoid being bitten, walked down the hill to the shores of Lake Quaboag and placed the raccoon and trap in our red canoe. My idea was to put the poor raccoon out of its misery by drowning it in the trap. After paddling out to deep water, I picked up the trap with the boat hook and held it over the side pitching the canoe dramatically to starboard. The canoe flipped over, sending me and the trapped raccoon into the water. We were both swallowed by Lake Quaboag's murky depths, but I was the only one to eventually rise back to the surface. After that, I executed rabid raccoons in the safer confines of a watering trough in the cow pasture.

The rabies epidemic killed large numbers of raccoons, but they have made a modest comeback in recent years. We are beginning to see healthy raccoons on their nightly jaunts when they come near lighted areas looking for food. We are respectful and even pleased to see them again, but with one caveat. Our American bald eagle nest is over seventy feet from the ground, but even at that height we still have to protect it from these agile marauders. A four-foot collar of stainless sheet metal has been securely installed at the base of the great white pine. So far the raccoons have been kept at bay.

EVERYONE I KNOW has had to deal with mice infestations. These creatures not only have found a way to penetrate the foundations, walls and doors of every building at *Oakholm*, but they also seem to delight in living in bird houses in the winter and messing them up. Anyone who lives in the country and claims to have no trouble with mice is in some strange state of denial. In fact the problems with these varmints are so many and so varied and so well known that I will not linger on them. Methods of eliminating them are also well known—mouse traps, sticky paper, poisons. All are unpleasant but unfortunately essential to keep a country house from being completely overrun and destroyed.

While visiting an uncle in Sweden in 1928 when I was eleven, I was introduced to a unique way of keeping these varmints under control. My uncle owned and operated a large farm on which he raised beef, cattle and horses. Like all farmers, he had to keep down the rat and mice populations. He had a clever solution. He filled a large, uncovered barrel about a third full of water. He covered the surface of the water with pieces of cork and sprinkled grain on top. A board was then placed at an angle from the ground to the top of the barrel, extending slightly over it. Mice and rats, smelling the grain, climbed the board to the top of the barrel and fell into the water. They could not escape, because the walls of the barrel were too smooth for them to get any traction to climb out. Every morning the night's catch was removed and buried and more grain was sprinkled on the floating cork. Like most eleven-year old boys, I secretly liked ghoulish and macabre things, and I never forgot my uncle's method for catching and executing rodents.

We introduced this "highly technical" system at *Oakholm* because we were naturally wary about setting traps and using poisons that might harm resident and visiting cats, dogs, birds and—most importantly—grandchildren. The barrel has been replaced by a steel rubbish can and the pieces of cork are cut up wine corks supplied by friendly tipplers. Like Bluebeard, the pirate who drowned his enemies by making them "walk the plank," we are doing likewise with mice. The difference is that Bluebeard forced his prisoners to jump. In our case, mice jump voluntarily to their demise in the rubbish can.

Living on and around the main house at *Oakholm*, as well as in barns, sheds, and trees, are hundreds, maybe thousands, of bats. The local variety has a small mouse-like body, beady black eyes and little rounded ears that stand straight up. Membrane-like wings attached to legs and arms spread to about six or seven inches and permit the bat to fly amazingly well in its search for food. This nocturnal animal primarily eats mosquitoes and other night flying insects which it catches in its little, toothy mouth. Our local bat eats about a third of its total weight in mosquitoes and flying insects every day.

Scientists wondered for years how bats, whose eyesight is very poor, could catch fast and evasive insects so easily, especially flying insects. In the 1940s scientists discovered that bats used "echolocation" to catch their prey and maneuver around trees and other objects. In flight, bats emit high-pitched sounds, undetectable to humans, which bounce off insects or objects and return to their highly sensitive ears. These returning sound waves, or echoes, are more accurate than eyesight and allow the bat to catch anything—or, if necessary, avoid anything. I remember watching a group of my fraternity brothers at Amherst armed with tennis rackets, canoe paddles, and butterfly nets chasing after one poor little bat throughout the common rooms of the fraternity house. The bat avoided all the blows aimed at him and eventually flew unscathed through an open door to the safety of the night outside. Though the bat escaped, the interior of the fraternity house did not, and the four bat chasers were properly fined for damaged furniture, broken lamps, and destroyed pictures. Thereafter, when the roll was called at fraternity functions, the letters B.C. were added to the names of the ignominious foursome, branding them forever as "Bat Chasers."

At *Oakholm*, hundreds of bats spend their daylight hours squeezed under the individual slate shingles on the roofs that cover all the buildings. Father insisted that all the roofs be slate to protect the structures from burning particles emitted from chimneys or sparks from forest fires. As yet, none of these roofs has been damaged by the bats. Window shutters

Bats emerge from behind shutters at Oakholm
as they're sprayed with water (2007)

are another matter. Bats like to live behind them, and their excretions eventually rot the shutters and the wood shingles or clapboards behind them. Additionally, an unattractive stain forms below. Since none of us wishes to harm the bats because of the millions of mosquitoes they eat, we decided that water sprayed over the tops of the shutters would make them uncomfortable enough to move elsewhere. It worked. When we first tried it, seventy-three bats crawled out of the top of one shutter and flew off in all directions to avoid the water and the sunlight. Some swooped close to me standing with the hose, but fortunately their echolocation devices were working perfectly and I was never touched.

In fairness to them, bats should really not be classified as varmints. Their appetite for mosquitoes helps control the population of these nefarious insects. In fact, rather than trying to extinguish them, we should help bats by either providing them with good living accommodations—special bat houses attached to trees—or by giving them clear access to an old shed or barn. Despite their fearsome reputation, New England bat species rarely bite human beings or domestic animals. If a bat inadvertently gets into your house, turn all the lights on and open a door or window at night. It will fly outside as quickly as it can.

Bram Stoker in his stories about Dracula, the blood-sucking vampire, describes vampires that fly as bats from place to place searching for human prey. These stories and Eastern European folklore have given bats a bad name. We all have friends who fear them. But of all the varmints described above, it is the bats whom we encourage to "hang around"—especially, in places approved by the human residents.

Foxes and Cats

A FEW YEARS AGO, OAKHOLM was overrun with cats. At the time, there were nine who lived in various barns and outbuildings. There were marmalade cats, black cats, bob-tailed cats, tiger cats, lazy fat cats, and trim hunting cats. These felines were fed a mixture of powdered milk and dried cat food in a large, rubber dish located in our central hay barn where it was available to all. The cats, like people, ate at different times in a proper pecking order, but usually in pairs or in threes. The dish was replenished daily.

Cat feeding was a rather routine affair until one foggy morning in late spring when all hell broke loose. Three baby foxes were seen lapping up the cat food, while the cats kept their distance, watching warily until the newcomers had finished. Three days later, the cats and the little fox cubs were eating simultaneously out of the same dish.

It did not take us long to figure out what brought the three little animals to the cat dish. Their dead mother was found on the road nearby, having been run over by an automobile. Foxes and cats, as if in a Peaceable Kingdom, ate and lived together harmoniously during May, June, and July. The foxes could be seen at mealtime, and played together in our orchard with little fear of humans. It was fun to watch them. But, in mid-August, a major change occurred. The foxes were no longer seen at the cat dish, and we noticed that fewer cats were eating there also. The lazy fat cat was missing and so was the bob-tailed cat. We soon discovered that the dietary habits of the foxes had changed from cat food to cats. Obviously, those foxes were undeterred by the old adage, "Don't bite the hand that feeds you!"

Hats

OUR FAMILY HAS always loved hats. Upon entering the main house at *Oakholm*, most visitors are attracted to a stairway wall directly ahead that is blessed with a collection of etchings and drawings by Anders Zorn, Carl Larson, Frank Benson, and J.M. Whistler. Much as we love those pictures, our own family is drawn instead to see what new additions have been made to a hat collection housed in a ten-foot square, windowed closet under an archway next to another door that leads to a wonderful playroom in the basement.

Currently, about seventy-five hats are piled helter-skelter on hooks and several shelves in the closet as well as on a hat rack, several lamps and a commode nearby. Every hat is different. The hats are of no particular period or type or from any special country. How did the collection begin? No one remembers for sure, but the catalyst may have been a business trip to Latin America some years ago.

Marianne and I travelled to Mexico with a group of twenty or so businessmen and their wives sponsored by David Rockefeller and the Pan American Union. For years, David, who was then President of Chase Bank, had organized meetings and symposia to improve business relations and trade with countries south of our border. While we were in Mexico City, Marianne was invited to attend a lunch and garden party by the wife of one of our Mexican counterparts. The hostess turned out to be Merle Oberon, a former movie star of the first magnitude. Her starring roles included *Wuthering Heights* with Laurence Olivier. Marianne was very impressed with Merle's beauty and also her hat, elegantly crafted as it was, in straw with a broad-brim, royal blue ribbons and an arrangement of cloth daffodils. When Marianne complimented her on the hat, Merle spontaneously took it off and graciously asked her to try it on. She quickly got the attention of the other guests, by announcing, "Look how much better Marianne looks in it than I do. I insist that she keep it!" That hat has a place of honor at *Oakholm* where it hangs on the door of the large closet.

Other hats in the collection were obtained at events given by interesting people and some family members. There is a black derby hat worn by my father when he had lunch with Calvin Coolidge at the White House. Father had known him when he served as governor of Massachusetts. Despite the many critics of Coolidge as president, Father admired his honesty, intelligence, his thrift with taxpayers' money, and his eloquent command of language. Coolidge wrote all his own speeches and proclamations. I particularly like this:

> The greatness of America lies around the hearthstone. If thrift and industry are taught there, and the example of self-sacrifice oft appears, if honor abide there, and high ideals, if there the building of fortune be subordinate to the building of character, Americans will live in security, rejoicing in abundant prosperity and good government at home, and in peace, respect, and confidence abroad. If these virtues be absent, no power can supply these blessings. Look well then to the Hearthstone; therein all hope for America lies.

From left, *In dinner hats—John Jeppson, Viking;*
Marianne's nephew, Sam Rea, Cat in the Hat;
Marianne Jeppson, jongleur (2003)

Marianne's Red Cross hat recalls her years of service during World War II when she drove a two-and-a-half ton truck to and from the front lines while attached to the 82nd Airborne Division and Patton's Third Army in France and Germany. My Navy hat is there reminding me of my four years of military duty.

In one corner of the shelf is a fitted leather case containing Grandfather's black high hat. I never saw him in it, but I can visualize this tall, patriarchal figure with a full white beard, moustache, and white wavy hair fringing the brim of that hat. I can see him doffing it to the ladies with a graceful flourish.

The last "boater" worn by my father, is also there. Boaters were flat crowned, straight brimmed, oval hats made with stiff straw and decorated, in this case, with a black ribbon around the crown. Properly attired men folk bought new ones in late spring every year and dispensed with them in favor of felt fedoras in the fall. In fact, friendly groups would often gather outside their clubs on the autumnal equinox and, when the signal was given, jump on their boaters. The stiff straw easily broke into a multitude of pieces. Luckily, Father's last one survived.

Panama hats were also worn in summer and an excellent one graces our collection. They are long lasting hats, made of fine straw, usually of a natural, off-white color, with a good brim and a wide black band. We have seen them being manufactured underground in Yucatan caves by Mexicans who are the descendants of ancient Mayans. They were working underground to keep the straw material damp and flexible, thereby preventing the individual straws from breaking as they are woven.

One of Marianne's favorite hats is that of a student lawyer from the University of Padua in Italy. It is a round cap made of red felt with a beak-shaped visor about six inches long. Gold braid is used for embellishment. Marianne acquired it while spending a year at the University of Florence in Italy and claims that it took all her feminine wiles to pry it from the head of a reluctant Paduan law student.

Other varieties include witches' hats, berets that make the wearers look like pumpkins, a hat worn by a Chinese Mandarin, a Dr. Seuss hat, a multi-colored "jongleur"—or medieval juggler's hat—with tiny lights at the ends of the dangling tips, a toreador hat and many more.

The hat collection is not static, nor is it for viewing only. The hats are in constant use. Family and friends wear them, but only in one place, the dining room. At family dinners, or dinners with guests, everyone is told to visit the hat room to select a hat of their choice to wear at the table. Is this a silly *Oakholm* tradition? Yes it is, but it does remove inhibitions. It makes people laugh. It loosens tongues as effectively as a martini, maybe even two martinis. It makes bashful people relax. It encourages people to use their cameras. At my ninetieth birthday party in Worcester, some seventy people—all wearing odd hats of their own choosing—surprised me at a cocktail party made all the more lively by the festive headgear.

Hats even encourage people to sing, who haven't done so in years. Speaking of singing, every dinner at *Oakholm* is begun with a rousing rendition of the Doxology, "Praise God from whom all blessings flow." I think God Himself (or Herself) must chuckle when He sees and hears an assemblage of normally serious and dignified people, singing to Him in unusual hats.

John Jeppson's 90th Birthday Party invitation (2006)

Businesses

WE HAVE ALWAYS GROWN raspberries at *Oakholm* for our own family's consumption. They do well in our temperate climate and thrive in relatively thin soils. In 1998 we noticed that the local market was flourishing. Prices were reasonably high, and local nurseries were producing fruit from excellent, disease-free plants. So we took the plunge, and decided to plant, raise, and sell raspberries at *Oakholm*.

The location we selected was in a field to the north of the farmhouse, close to a small pond which could be used to irrigate the raspberry bushes in dry weather. The eastern edge of the field was bounded by Lake Road, the public road which bisects the farm, thus providing an access point for customers, in case we decided to operate as a "pick your own" operation. As the name implies, "pick your own" customers pick the ripe berries for themselves, usually with minimal supervision. When they are done picking, they pay either by volume or by weight. So far, we have done all our own picking and sold our berries through our neighbor Mark Ledoux, who sells local and organically grown fruit and vegetables. His stand is simple but attractive, consisting of heavy, unpainted planks on sawhorses with a shed roof covering part of it. It is shaded by great sugar maples. Since his stand is usually unattended, a sign displays the prices and customers slip money through a slot in the top of an old, steel five-gallon milk can. The system is based on trust but, just in case, the can is filled halfway with concrete to dissuade any-one from running off with it.

The season is over when the first frost hits, usually late September. Then we cut the canes of the raspberry plants to the ground, because next year's berries will all be produced on new canes ripe for picking in August. We do this in order to produce berries after most of our competitors have ended their season. However, this approach has risks. An early frost could be disastrous, for example. There is also the chance of heavy rains in late August or September, and if the rain lasts too long, fungal diseases may attack the plants. So far, we have been lucky. During late summer and fall last year, we produced three hundred pints from our raspberry rows. We are now adding more bushes, including new and better varieties, that will be appreciated by strangers lucky enough to buy *Oakholm* raspberries.

PRODUCING BLUEBERRIES WAS another business we thought we could easily add to our list at *Oakholm*. Wild blueberry bushes, both high and low-bush types, were already flourishing when we first arrived in 1925. Many of these had been shaded out by the white pines, oaks, and maples that have grown into 21st century giants since the hurricane of 1938. As we did with our raspberries, we decided to locate the blueberry patch close to *Oakholm*'s main entrance to make it accessible to customers. Over a period of several years, we planted excellent high-bush plants, hoping to establish a "pick your own" business. We foresaw taking two years to establish our new bushes before beginning to harvest in late summer. As with our raspberries, we chose late season varieties in order to have less competition from neighboring growers, most of whom featured mid-season varieties.

We took excellent care of our plants. They were planted in proper-sized holes, and their roots were carefully spread out to receive quantities of peat moss and friable soil around them. Plenty of water was added at planting time and every few days thereafter to ensure that the roots would be well established. We placed wood chip mulch around each plant to retain moisture and to discourage weeds. Finally, we spread powdered 10-10-10 fertilizer over the mulch to feed the new plants. Moisture would gradually filter it down through the particles of silt to the fine, hair-like blueberry roots.

The plants flourished. They flowered prolifically, and each flower became a blueberry. The tiny green berries grew larger and larger until they ripened and began to turn blue. They were soon ready to be picked, and they were, but not by any "pick your own" customers. Animals beat us to the punch. First, birds raided the blueberry patch with cat birds taking the lead. We promptly put up black plastic netting over a bamboo structure to protect the berries. That took care of the bird problem. However, that was only the first wave of the animal attacks. Chipmunks burrowed under the nets, and ate virtually all of the remaining blueberries. We hope to solve this problem in the future, but so far we have been outwitted by the varmints. Needless to say, blueberries have yet to generate any farm income.

CHRISTMAS TREES have been planted at *Oakholm* almost from the very first years of our family's ownership of the place. Two or three were planted in several woodland locations and twenty were planted in a small clearing. The idea was to have enough for family and friends. The trees grew well and seeds from their cones started more seedlings. Soon there were more trees reaching Christmas tree size than the family could use. This led to Christmas tree parties. Good friends were invited to these, bringing family with them—armed with saws, ropes, bungies, etc.—for cutting their own trees and tying them on top of their cars.

The weather was usually cold and, after cars had been loaded with trees, we all looked forward to hot mulled cider and Swedish *Gløgg* in front of our big fireplace. The menu was always the same—baked beans, brown bread, coleslaw and apple pie. Otherwise polite, fastidious people were seen shovelling large portions of this provender into their hungry maws after all their laboring outdoors.

After several years the parties grew too large and some of our friends too old—including Marianne and me—to continue this type of entertainment. However, we began to think of raising Christmas trees commercially. There were several locations near the road and near the barns. These were gravelly areas that lacked good soil necessary for raising hay and other crops, but was fine for raising balsams, firs, spruces and pines. Being close to the road and barns, these areas would also be easy for customers to view, select and remove the trees they wanted to buy.

The die was cast in 1995. Paul and I put our heads together and decided to buy and plant one hundred balsam seedlings. These were planted in April of that year and each year thereafter we added enough to reach a total of two thousand in 2005. Since then we have planted

Christmas trees (2007)

just enough to replace those which were sold or died from disease or drought. It takes ten years to produce a six-foot tree, so that last year, 2006, became the first good sales year. You will remember that our first planting of a hundred trees was in 1995. We have found that most people want a tree that is six feet or more in height. Although balsams with their beautiful aroma constitute the majority of our trees, we have also planted Scotch pine, Concolor fir, Douglas fir, Fraser fir, and white spruce. There is a variety to suit every taste.

We got the bright idea of selling sprigs of holly to tree customers and found there was quite a demand for them. In the future we plan to put together holly with pine cones and laurel for decorations.

To attract customers who usually bring children and to put them in the spirit of the holiday, Paul's daughter, Jasmin, has made a unique manger with Christ child, Mary and Joseph fashioned from burlap and old clothing. Around the manger are live turkeys, sheep, and calves. Classic Christmas carols and sacred music play in the background. We are impressed with those who come to select their trees. They take the time necessary to get just what they want. Quite often there are differences of opinion, and a few need help cutting the trees, carrying them and tying them to their cars. All in all, we enjoy meeting those who come, but it takes a lot of time on the weekends between Thanksgiving and Christmas. To date, advertising for our trees has been minimal. Signs on the road, one a mile north, the other a mile south, plus one ad in the *Brookfield Citizen*, a monthly local paper, is all we do to promote the business. We will do more advertising in the future, as we hope to sell more trees each year.

We have found that growing Christmas trees is surprisingly labor intensive. Planting seedlings takes time, and the soil must be prepared for them by removing brush and weeds. A special planting spade is used to plant three year old seedlings in holes six to eight inches in depth. These are planted in rows five-feet apart. Every so often a ten-foot row is planted to allow larger vehicles to enter the area. Grass and weeds need to be cut with a mowing machine three or four times a summer to prevent them from stunting the growth of the young trees. The most time-consuming job is pruning, usually begun about three or four years after planting, when the young trees are beginning to grow vigorously. This takes skilled use of shears and clippers to produce the symmetrical shapes desired by the market.

Although it takes years of hard work to raise good, saleable Christmas trees, it is a satisfactory use of time, as well as good use of marginal land. But not much land. Our two thousand trees and the roads leading to them use less than an acre and a half. The trees are a beautiful sight to see in all stages of their growth, even the birds like them and nest in them. They are a renewable resource. Finally, they bring happiness and joy to the families that buy them.

At Oakholm, we lease our hay fields; we produce a few gallons of maple syrup; we raise a few turkeys, and a couple of steers. These each produce income, but not very much. Most of what we do is labor intensive. Paul, our manager and man of all work, has all he can do to handle the varied businesses we now operate. The question facing us is what can we do to make this small, beautiful New England farm self-sustaining in order to prevent it from ultimately being gobbled up by developers or transformed into a golf course for the benefit of a few old duffers like me who would spend most of their time at the nineteenth hole?

Maintenance

FROM TIME TO TIME, members of our family and friends have taken on maintenance projects at *Oakholm*. The principal job has been brush-cutting seedlings and sprouts—oak, maple, white pine, wild cherry and brambles—which are the main culprits found on the edges of fields. The young trees overwhelm blueberry bushes, blot out pathways, and infiltrate plantings of rhododendron, laurel, and dogwood. They often force themselves into areas too close to farm buildings. Most of these invaders grow one or two feet per year, and if they are not cut and controlled early, will take much more labor to remove as saplings with thicker stems and trunks. After the brush is cut, it has to be picked up and hauled to a neat pile or to a brush dump. Long-handled clippers, saws, and axes are the usual tools. When it comes to assigning tasks and paying family members who only have time to work on weekends or vacations, we point out an area needing attention and establish a price based on the number of hours we estimate it will take to finish cutting the brush and hauling it away. This eliminates the problem of timekeeping and enables the family worker to arrange his or her own time to accommodate labor among recreational activities, like swimming, fishing, tennis, or just plain relaxing.

More than fifty years ago, Marianne and I had a brilliant idea for removing brush that was threatening to overwhelm the farm. We decided to invite twenty strong and healthy friends out to *Oakholm* to cut it. We would provide a keg of beer for them in order to renew their vigor and enthusiasm in case they became tired or bored with the work. Marianne would cook up some wonderful vittles as a reward for their work, and a prize would be given to the person who cut the most brush. The prize was to be a young, five-foot hemlock dug from our woods. Invitations went out. The great day arrived, and so did our burly friends. The weather that late September day was perfect—not too hot, not too cold—just right for cutting brush. The uniform of the day was a T-shirt and blue jeans. Each of the guests brought their own tools and was anxious to get to work. We barely had time to show them what to cut, let alone how to go about it. The weekend rang with the blows of axes, the whine of saws, and the cheerful voices of young men and women. Birds were frightened, chipmunks stayed in their burrows, and earth worms moved to lower levels to escape the heavy tread of forty large feet.

As the afternoon wore on, progress slowed and an ever larger group lingered around the water, soda, and beer. Eventually work ground to a complete halt. Dexterous manual labor gave way to consuming the turkey, beef, vegetables, and ice cream that Marianne had provided. In the murkiness of the late afternoon and evening, it appeared that great accomplishments had taken place. The award to the champion brush cutter had been made with appropriate ceremony and good fellowship reigned until late into the night.

In the morning sun of the next day, Marianne and I inspected the work done by our muscular friends. We were appalled. Most of the brush had been cut too high up on the stems and trunks, leaving sharp-pointed stubs to trip hikers and wound the unwary. As a result, we had to re-cut the long brush stubs left by our friends back to ground level. We were at it for days. As some people might say, "Too many cooks spoil the broth." As *Oakholm's* Marianne said, "Food and drink make workers stink!"

AN ONGOING MAINTENANCE job at *Oakholm* is painting. Occasionally, our progeny take on a major painting job, but not often. It's hard to fit a painting job into a short time span. Also, some otherwise talented family members are not very good at painting. They are either too sloppy or too slow. One painter, however, deserves particular recognition: our oldest grandson, Craig Stout, who painted the chain-link backstops on our tennis court when he was sixteen years old. Aluminum metal paint was used on both sides of the backstops. In the process, Craig covered himself, as well as the fencing, with bright aluminum. As he covered more and more of his body and face, he took on the distinct appearance of the Tin Woodman of *The Wonderful Wizard of Oz.*

For fifteen years, most painting was done by a contractor, Bill Williams, a dependable, local painter—except when he over-imbibed. He "tied one on" once a month or so and would go missing for several days. He was also highly susceptible to the lure of the spring trout season or the fall deer season, temptations for which I was more sympathetic. We paint our twelve buildings every seven years, not all at once, but staggered, so that three or fewer are painted in any given year. Until World War II, exterior paint lasted almost twice as long as it does today, because of its durable but deadly lead base. Painters using it daily had short life spans and young children were particularly affected by lead poisoning—animals, too. At *Oakholm*, young calves grazing in an area surrounded by a newly-painted wooden fence, became sick and soon died because they licked the fence posts and rails with their small rough tongues.

Appropriately, the use of lead paint is now banned. Unfortunately, none of our present-day paints lasts as long outdoors as the old lead-based varieties. We have tried every type produced by every manufacturer—water-based or oil-based—and none has lasted more than several years. Paul has come up with a different approach to painting. Instead of painting whole buildings or even the complete side of a building, he and whoever helps him simply touches up every spot needing paint anywhere on all twelve *Oakholm* buildings. The buildings are inspected regularly and every spot that has peeled or cracked is scraped, sanded and primed. The trick is to blend in the color of the final coat with the old painted surface surrounding it. Fortunately, Paul is a master at blending the old with the new.

In the spring of 2006, we devised an entirely new approach to painting at *Oakholm* that we initiated in the fall. We selected the south wall of the horse barn as our target, an area about eighty-feet high at the peak of the roof and about fifty-feet wide at the base. The new approach involved removing the paint down to the bare wood, and then painting two coats of a very special and expensive paint. Removing all the paint and getting down to bare wood proved to be a horrendous job. We calculated that the seventy-five year old barn had been painted on average every seven or so years. Scraping off eleven layers of paint by hand proved nearly impossible. Next, we tried halogen heat lamps. This

The south wall of the horse barn, freshly painted (2006)

was too slow and too dangerous, since the technique required the use of both hands which is very unsafe on a ladder. We put up some staging, but that was difficult because of the steep hill on which the horse barn sits. Finally, Paul and his partner, Lee, were able to erect reasonably secure staging that allowed them to use motorized paint shavers with carbide teeth. They had to be careful not to scar the wooden surface, and regardless of how careful they were, the shaver would occasionally take out a chunk of wood which necessitated vigorous sanding. Finally, as Christmas approached, preparation was finished, and the first coat of paint was on.

After following the program closely and inspecting the job at various stages, the paint company assured us that the job would last a lifetime. But what is a lifetime? The rest of mine is unlikely to exceed ten years. On the other hand, that of my youngest grandchild should be at least seventy-five years. We have yet to pin down the paint company on specifics.

Although the job appears to be successful, one minor tragedy should be noted. Two of our twenty-two turkeys flew out of their yard and landed just below the south end of the horse barn. They were soon caught and put back where they belonged. In a few days they began to limp and were unable to keep up with the rest of the flock. The vet was called and found that they had contracted lead poisoning from paint chips that had been scraped and removed from the building. The veterinarian said that the two turkeys would not harm humans if cooked and eaten because any lead they had ingested would be concentrated in the bones, not the meat. Despite his assurances, the two turkeys did not grace anyone's Thanksgiving table.

Pastures and Woods

THE PRINCIPAL WOOD lot at *Oakholm* is about seventy acres in size and was a cow pasture when we first purchased the farm. Most of it is on a hillside facing east with a beautiful view over Lake Quaboag and the hills beyond. It is dotted with a few big sugar maples, white pines, oaks and old dead chestnuts. They are surrounded by their progeny in the form of seedlings and saplings.

Stone walls crisscross the area denoting the boundaries of former fields. I have often thought of the early settlers who pried the stones out of the ground with wooden levers, iron crowbars and pickaxes, then pushed them onto "stone boats" pulled by oxen, and dumped them off at the right location. Stone boats were about six or seven-feet long, and four or five-feet wide, and built of heavy planks held together by cross pieces of heavy wood front and back. To prevent the boat from digging into the ground when pulled by oxen, a piece of iron or steel was built around the front edge. The stones were built into walls to keep cattle, sheep and pigs in place.

Before working on the granite stones, those intrepid, colonial farmers had to cut down the trees, remove the stumps, and build their cabins and sheds. Plowing, harrowing, seeding, and harvesting were the final jobs for these agrarian titans who produced the food and lumber enabling our colonies to exist and, ultimately, to flourish.

On our hillside pasture three rocks were too large and too heavy to be moved. We have adopted one of them—a large, granite rectangle, seven-feet high and eight-feet wide—as our favorite picnic spot. It is temporarily off limits because a heavy infestation of poison ivy vines has recently overwhelmed it.

Before trees covered it, high-bush blueberries were plentiful on the hillside, and in season, women and children armed with baskets and pails picked the tasty berries. Since the area was also a pasture, our Guernsey cows presented a concern for the berry pickers. Cows are curious animals. Occasionally, they ambled close to the berries. At one time a cow, uttering a series of low-pitched "moos," put her large horned head right through a bush where Anna Skoog was busily picking berries. Even though Guernsey cows are notably tame, the sight of the large brown and white head within a few inches of her own would cause any self-respecting lady to panic. Anna let out a shriek and spilled her blueberries as she leapt backward. Eventually, she calmed down, and the rest of the pickers dissolved in laughter.

As time progressed, the cows were pastured elsewhere. The seedlings on the hillside grew into saplings, and the saplings matured into sizeable trees. The pasture became a seventy-acre forest. For years, trees were allowed to grow naturally. Only an occasional dead, rotten or deformed tree was removed for firewood for our *Oakholm* fireplaces. The very large trees were victims of the hurricane of 1938, but the seedlings and saplings were flexible enough to survive the 125 mile per hour winds and eventually flourished.

By 1990, many of these were large enough to be harvested on a selective basis. We turned to an experienced forester licensed by the Commonwealth of Massachusetts for advice. He developed a forest management plan for us that involved the selective cutting of trees to produce income from logs for lumber and firewood. It also provided both open spaces for tree seeds to germinate as well as attractive tree and groundcover to attract birds and small mammals that spread the seeds. We also followed good forest management practice by leaving slash—branches too small for firewood—on the ground to provide cover for wildlife and ultimately to rot into soil-enriching compost.

The American chestnut (*Castanea dentata*) was a major tree in our forests until hit by the deadly fungus disease in the early 1900s. It was a fast-growing tree that reached an average height of a hundred feet. Its nuts were edible and good-tasting and provided food for deer and wild turkeys. Its wood was longer-lasting than any other, and was beautifully grained. Losing this tree was a national disaster. Chestnut shoots are still growing from old roots, but they invariably die from the disease when very young. Beginning in about 1980, however, chestnuts in many locations around the country began to last longer and grow larger. At *Oakholm*, several chestnut trees have grown to a seven-inch caliper and a twenty-five foot height and produced nuts before being girdled and killed by the fungus. Fortunately, a major effort is underway headed by the American Chestnut Foundation to bring back this great tree by crossing it with the disease-resistant Chinese chestnut. A grove has been planted at Tower Hill Botanic Garden, the great horticultural center run by the Worcester County Horticultural Society in Boylston, Massachusetts. Chestnut nurseries have been established in many locations. Perhaps in fifty to a hundred years, disease-free American chestnuts will be thriving everywhere again, producing wonderful shade, food, and lumber.

The Eagles Have Landed

ON A BRIGHT MAY afternoon in 2001, Marianne and I were raking up thousands of pine cones which had fallen from three great white pines located near our family clubhouse—the *J House*—on the western shore of Lake Quaboag. We cursed the day in the spring of 1926 when my father and I had planted the three pine seedlings. Seventy-five years later, they had become one hundred foot giants. We wondered why we had protected them with lightning rods when they created so much miserable work year after year. Not only did we have to collect their sticky cones, we also had to pick up twigs and branches after every storm and scrape needles off the roofs—needles which also clogged the filters in the nearby swimming pool.

While in the depths of negative ruminations about the trees, we had a visitation that completely changed our outlook. Looking up from our labor, we saw an unfamiliar, uniformed man striding quickly down the long hill from the main house with Paul Benjamin, who was struggling to keep up. In a moment, we were introduced to the tall, red-haired, athletic man who breathlessly introduced himself as Brad Blodget, Chief Ornithologist for the Commonwealth of Massachusetts. "You have eagles," he shouted at us, "American bald eagles—building a nest on your property! Yours is nest Number 12 in the state, and the only one in Worcester County. A young pair is building a nest over there."

As he spoke, he pointed to another group of pines in a wood lot about three hundred yards away. We saw nothing unusual about the trees until he led us to a point on the lake shore where we could view them from another angle. Sure enough, we could see a dense area in one of the trees that proved to be an eagle's nest under construction. A bird watcher across the lake had called Blodget after seeing eagles flying regularly around the lake. Using his telescope, he had eventually zeroed in on the nest from a spot on the opposite shore.

Brad was pleased that the eagles had set up housekeeping on land owned by responsible people—technically on our daughter Muffy's property which was adjacent to our own—who would help him monitor the great birds. As he talked, and as if on cue, we were thrilled to see one of the eagles flying across the lake toward the nest with a good-sized bass in its talons. Marianne and I were astonished that there were only twelve eagle nests in all of Massachusetts. Five were near the Quabbin Reservoir, five were nestled along the Connecticut River, and one of the two others—was right in front of us on Lake Quaboag. We were delighted.

Bald eagles are magnificent birds distinguished by their dark bodies and pure white heads, necks and tails. Their eyes, sharp curved beaks and legs are golden yellow. Their legs are armed with skinny, black talons. As young adults, the eagles are dark brown and do not acquire their white plumage until they are four or five years of age. The female is larger and heavier than the male. She has a wingspan of six to eight feet, her mate's being nearer to six feet. Bald eagles live twelve to twenty years in the wild, but there are some cases where they have reached thirty years in captivity. One source mentions a fifty-year old specimen.

Eagles appear to be slow fliers, circling widely over lakes and rivers. When hunting, however, they are capable of high speeds and are able to out-fly ducks, geese, and often swans. When diving to catch their prey, it is estimated that they reach speeds in excess of one hundred miles per hour. Our foremost local ornithologist, E. H. Forbush, in his *Birds of Massachusetts*, published in 1925, describes the flight of the eagle:

> I well recall the day when, as an impressionable lad, I first saw the Bald Eagle wheeling majestically up the sky until it rose to a height almost beyond the compass of my straining vision and there—a mere speck in the blue—it sailed away until it vanished in the vast spaces of the upper air. The great bird had been fishing in Podunk Pond (Lake Quaboag) in Brookfield and, startled by the sound of my gun, had passed away from the mundane scene apparently as lightly as a drifting cloud.

Eagles do not mate until they are nearly five-years old. Their honeymoon is a harsh one, occupied for the most part by finding a proper location for their nest and then constructing it. Since they are primarily fishermen, they search for a tall, strong tree with a good view over a body of water—a river, a lake or the sea—where food is plentiful. The pair build their nest during their first year together, but eggs are not laid until the second. There are rarely more than three.

Eagle nests are huge, four feet or more in length and width. They are made of sticks which can be several feet long and more than an inch thick. Since eagles normally use the same nest year after year, and add to it annually, an old nest can grow to over eight-feet long, and can be very deep and weigh over a ton. The *Oakholm* nest was built in a white pine at a height of about seventy feet. At four feet from the ground, the circumference of the tree is nearly eleven feet. We needed to calculate the circumference so the state could supply us with enough sheet metal to wrap around the tree trunk to prevent raccoons from climbing up to the nest to eat the eggs.

In 2001, it was estimated that only ten eaglets fledged in Massachusetts with births occurring in just five of the twelve nests—a low yield. However, the average pair breeds and produces young over a ten-year period. Assuming an average of one and a half fledglings a year per nest, and the addition of one or two nests per year, the outlook for eagles in our neighborhood was not too bad. I expect to see about fifteen or more eagles flying around Brookfield in another ten years. Since we first discovered our eagles, we have been casting our eyes in their direction every time we venture outside the house, but we do not see them very often. Their strength and speed permit them to cover great distances, so they could be almost anywhere in New England. Eagles in Massachusetts rarely migrate, but in the winter, they move from frozen lakes to open water areas such as the Connecticut River. They often roost in protected groves with other eagles. I assume that these are the spots where unattached young males and females appraise each other as a prelude to mating.

In mid-October 2001, a grandson and I saw one of a pair of eagles being harassed by a passel of eight or ten crows. But the majestic preda-tors were not really bothered by them. An occasional flap of a giant wing was enough to keep any crow at bay. We have seen small birds, darting at eagles, but they do not seem to mind. During one sighting, an eagle launched out of the nesting area and flew several circles over the lake. Its mate soon followed. They kept flying higher and higher until they both disappeared into the blue sky overhead. Although we could not see them, they could easily see us after disappearing from our sight. A bald eagle sees eight times better than a human—they can spot a mouse a mile away and a rabbit two miles.

Eagles have long captivated our imagination. Sumerians, Egyptians, Romans and early Christians all were fascinated with the eagle. The eagle has become a long standing symbol of America, despite having prominent detractors. James Audubon considered the eagle "a rank coward" and Benjamin Franklin preferred the turkey, not the eagle, as our national bird.

Closer to home, in the mid 1880s, E. H. Forbush, in his *Birds of Massachusetts*, wrote about a pet eagle owned by a former citizen of Worcester:

> The late C. B. Pratt, whose fondness for pets of all sorts was notorious, kept in a large, flying cage a Bald Eagle, which was said to have been taken from a nest on Lake Washacum in Sterling in the days when that region was heavily and extensively wooded. More or less meat, food for the eagle, lay about on the ground under the eagle's tree. This often attracted stray cats. The eagle had a peculiar method of killing cats. When it noted one of the beasts within its wire enclosure, it descended by stealthy hops from branch to branch of his leafless tree. Finally, it dropped with a heavy flop on the cat's back, seizing the animal by the spine and the neck with its great claws in such a way that the victim was immediately disabled and soon killed.

A self-made man, Charles Blake Pratt served as mayor of Worcester for three years and was known for his good works, including the development of the street railway system and the installation of drains and sewers that made it possible to build homes and factories in what is now Quinsigamond Village.

Bald eagles are making a comeback in spite of everything humans have done to make them extinct. They have been blamed as dangerous marauders and, for generations, have been hunted and shot. Yet, it is almost impossible to find references to eagles killing domestic fowl or animals. Unless they were stealing eggs or fledglings, humans have almost never been attacked. Eagles rarely kill other birds and their diet is principally fish and carrion, and, to a lesser extent, rodents and rabbits. Fish and small animals tainted with DDT did more to diminish the eagle populations than anything else. When ingested by female eagles, the DDT laced fish caused eagle eggs to form with shells too weak to protect the young embryos. Of course, the biggest threat to eagles has been humans. Inadvertently or otherwise, we have destroyed much of the eagle habitat. Urban sprawl, malls, houses and camps around lakes and rivers, and the cutting of tall trees have destroyed major nesting sites.

By 1968, the eagle population in the lower forty-eight states had diminished to 417 pairs, and was finally declared an endangered species, protected by federal law. The fine for shooting an eagle is currently $10,000. All dead eagles, including feathers, are the legal property of Native American tribes. Nests must not be disturbed. In addition, scientists and conservationists have worked hard, not only to protect the bird, but also to develop breeding programs to increase the population.

Now there are estimated to be several thousand breeding pairs in the United States.

In March 2003, Larry Hatstat, our eagle watcher on the other side Lake Quaboag, noted that our eagle pair had returned to its nest from their winter habitat. We do not know where they spend the winter, but it is probably not too far south. Our hard winter climate does not faze them. The issue is ice. Eagles need to be near a river or seacoast where fish, their major food source, is available to them. Two feet of ice on Lake Quaboag in the winter of 2003 forced our pair to spend the winter elsewhere. Eagles often perch near one another in winter and willingly share a good fishing hole together.

It was late March when the ice on Lake Quaboag finally broke up. Our bald eagles returned to the same nest they had built three years earlier, and immediately went to work. The pair concentrated on strengthening the basic structure of the nest by adding more long sticks and lining it with a soft pliable material—grass leaves and moss—to provide a proper place for eggs and, ultimately, eaglets

Our eagles had spent their first year at Lake Quaboag in 2001 building their original nest. We had expected eggs and eaglets a year later but no progeny appeared. We theorized that the female was too young to produce eggs, since she did not possess full adult plumage. Some of her feathers still appeared to be a teen-aged brown.

In April of 2003, a change occurred in our pair's behavior. They were no longer working on their nest. We no longer saw both eagles flying around, but instead noticed that one eagle always stayed in the nest. It took the female a few days to produce her eggs, followed by an incubation period of about thirty-five days. During incubation, both the male and female took turns warming the eggs while the mate searched for food. We were convinced that the eggs had hatched when we saw another behavioral change. One eagle continued to stay close to the nest, but only occasionally sat in the nest itself. The other eagle busily fished for food. The pair often spent time together just outside the nest which indicated that newborn eaglets might have arrived. We were cautiously optimistic that our pair had grown into a family, but we refused to celebrate until we could see the eaglets with our own eyes.

The Division of Fisheries and Wildlife of Massachusetts once again came into the picture. They notified us in late May that they planned to come to our "eagle tree" in June to determine whether there were young in the nest. If so, they were prepared to band them. Using powerful telescopes, sharp-eyed specialists can learn the identity of a banded bird by reading markings, one federal and the other state.

We were very pleased to have the experts return. On the appointed day, everyone involved gathered in a field one hundred or so yards from the eagle tree. The regional heads of Fisheries and Wildlife for Central and Western Massachusetts were both present as well as an alpine climber, a photographer, an ornithologist, several technicians, a few close neighbors, and various members of our family. The equipment included alpine climbing equipment, cameras, a canoe in case an eaglet fell in the water, and chairs with slanted backs to allow us octogenarians to sit comfortably while surveying the goings-on seventy feet above us. We resembled an African safari in search of big game.

As we started across the field, the two adult eagles became alarmed and circled around us uttering piercing cries. At the base of the tree, the professionals went to work. An alpine mechanism similar to a mechanical

Lowering an eaglet from its nest (2003)

slingshot was used to shoot a small beanbag over a strong branch of a tree next to the nest. A light line was attached to the beanbag, which allowed the alpinist to pull a stout rope over the branch and back down to the ground. Properly fastened, the alpine rope was now ready for the climber to use it to pull himself up near the nest. He ascended seventy feet to the nest very quickly, and immediately signaled that there was an eaglet in the nest. He scooped it up, placed it in a soft canvas bag and lowered it to the ground. The eaglet was removed from the bag and placed on my lap. It was one of the great thrills of my life to hold this little creature in my hands. Actually, the eaglet was not so little. At about four weeks of age, it already weighed six pounds, and had a wingspan of eighteen inches. Although the eaglet looked a bit like a plucked chicken, its noble head, fierce eyes, sharp beak and talons revealed a perfectly formed American bald eagle. The banding came next—a federal ID clipped around one leg, a state ID clipped around the other. I was pleased to see that the bands were loose, very light and would in no way hamper the bird during its lifetime After the eaglet was banded, it was quickly returned to its nest which seemed to please its parents. They had been flying furiously around the nest during the entire exercise. Some believe that adult birds will desert their young if they have been handled by humans, but our state experts assured us that this is an "old wives' tale." The loving attention shown our young eagle by its parents reassured us.

In addition to banding the eaglet and measuring it, the specialists examined the nest to determine from debris what food it had been fed. At the end of the day, the eaglet was pronounced a healthy specimen that resided near a robust food source and was the likely beneficiary of humans nearby who were concerned about its welfare. Even the pilots of seaplanes that routinely practice their takeoffs and landings on the lake have changed their flight plans to avoid disturbing the eagles and their nest.

Marianne and I next had the pleasure of observing the eaglet as it grew. We especially enjoyed watching it parade around the edge of the nest showing off its brown feathers. This color would not change into the striking black and white feathering of its parents for another five years. The eaglet was expected to fly at twelve to fourteen weeks. At ten weeks, our eaglet was hopping vigorously up and down in the nest, and actively flapping its young wings. Our patient observer across the lake saw the first flight by telescope on August 27 about fourteen

John Jeppson holding a newly banded bald eaglet (2003)

weeks after our eaglet's birth. Remarkably, it had become the size of its parents with a glorious, six-foot wingspan. The eaglet's first flights were wobbly and low. He preferred to perch on low branches and even fence posts rather than soar across the lake. The parents remained close at hand and continued to feed their clumsy progeny. By the onset of winter, our eaglet had become a practiced flyer and an effective hunter. In less than a year, it was essentially independent of its parents.

Unfortunately, 2004 was a sad one for our eagle pair. As we had a year earlier, we observed them preparing their nest for a new brood. Larry Hatstat, our eagle watcher, observed that by April they were incubating their eggs. The nest was never left vacant by the pair. But throughout the month of May, we saw no eaglet head appearing above the edge of the nest. This raised the question of whether or not an eaglet had hatched. To find out, a team from the Division of Fisheries and Wildlife returned to the eagle tree, and sent a climber up seventy feet to the nest again. Sadly, all he found was one cracked egg and a few broken pieces of a second egg. Although experts examined both the cracked egg and the broken pieces, no one could figure out what had happened.

Despite failing to produce more young in 2004, the adult pair remained near Lake Quaboag. In the fall of 2004, Larry—ever observant—noticed that the pair was spending more time in a pine grove about a quarter mile north of their original nest on our property. In December, he discovered that the eagles had established a new nest in a tall, white pine one hundred feet from the water's edge on the northwest shore of Lake Quaboag. By February 2005, Larry observed that a white eagle head could be seen continuously for more than a month—a sure sign that one or more eggs were in the nest. The female and male eagle took turns keeping the eggs warm for the thirty-five day incubation period. As at their earlier locations, a well-camouflaged aluminum sheet was placed around the base of the tree to prevent marauders like raccoons from climbing the tree. Once the incubation had ended, our observers began to see two small heads appearing above the edge of the nest from time to time. When Bill Davis of the Divison of Fisheries and Wildlife and his crew arrived to band the eaglets, there were not the expected pair. There were three eaglets.

By 2007, our eagles produced a total of nine eaglets in seven years. To keep the generations straight we have given them proper names, drawing from Shakespeare, Mother Goose and the Bible. We were so impressed by the resilience of one generation of three eaglets that we named them Shadrach, Meshach and Abednego after the three men who survived the fiery furnace in the Book of Daniel of the Old Testament.

Shadrach, Meshach and Abednego on and near their nest (2006)
Photo by Dan Cooper

Yankee Doodle et al

MARIANNE'S AND MY first dog was a Dalmatian named Yankee Doodle. We almost lost him as a puppy when he devoured a large quantity of birdseed. Thirsty from the dry seed, he drank several bowls of water and his stomach promptly swelled to many times its normal size. We rushed him to the vet where an emergency stomach pumping saved his life.

Yankee was an active dog with a distinct sense of humor and zest for living. On his own, he developed an indoor game, which he played frequently—especially when he had an audience. He would stand for a moment at the top of our curved stairway and then run down the carpeted steps as fast as he could, leaping over the last three. He would land with all four legs in a stiff, braced position on top of a scatter rug causing it to slide three or four feet. By shifting his weight, he could change the direction of his slide from right to left like a bobsled pilot.

Shortly after Marianne and I were married, Father gave her a green Ford coupe as a Christmas present. It arrived on our driveway with a large red bow on the hood. We had acquired Yankee just before the new car arrived and he was just as excited about the new coupe as Marianne. He immediately appropriated the small rear seat and for several days

Marianne with Yankee Doodle and Britta's dog, Duke (1949)

rode proudly behind Marianne. Eventually, however, his body weight depressed the seat cushion enough to create a space between seat and back. When Marianne stopped the car to let herself and the dog out, he stood up sharply, pinching his tail between the two cushions. He yelped with fright, thinking some large animal had attacked him. From then on he never rode in the rear seat again. Instead, he took over the front passenger seat where he rode even more proudly than before, with Marianne as chauffeur.

On one occasion, Yankee almost spoiled an evening dinner party. Marianne had prepared a special *smörgåsbord* or cold buffet—plates of sliced ham, beef, chicken, salmon, and cheese. Hot dishes and desserts were to be served after the arrival of the guests. While she and I were upstairs dressing for the occasion, Yankee surreptitiously made his way to the dining room, and delicately sampled each of the dishes. He only took one or two slices from each platter without moving the dish or wrinkling the tablecloth, hoping that his thievery would go unnoticed. Fortunately, Marianne replaced the losses before the party began.

Yankee was a self-taught retriever, or rather a "collector." When Worcester newsboys delivered rolled-up papers to doorsteps, Yankee picked up the newspapers of our seven neighbors and deposited them at our front door—one by one. He sometimes brought us outdoor chair cushions, which were often not returned because we couldn't find out where they came from. Marianne foiled his attempt at what would have been his crowning acquisition. Gazing dreamily out of a second story window on a clear summer day, she suddenly noticed Yankee pulling a baby carriage up the road. He moved it along by grabbing its wooden handle and tugging it by a series of jerks. With each tug, it moved about six inches, an arduous process. Marianne ran across the road to Yankee, and was horrified when she saw that the carriage was occupied. A very small baby was lying in it, apparently enjoying the ride. Marianne fortunately knew whose child and carriage it was, and immediately brought them back the eighty feet they had been dragged by Yankee. To this day, the baby's mother has never been apprised of her baby's journey with Yankee Doodle fifty-five years ago.

Although we knew Dalmatians shed, we never realized how much until Marianne and I were about to go out one evening to have dinner with my superior at Norton Company, Milton P. Higgins. She wore a long, black taffeta dress as befitted a formal dinner with the boss. As she descended the stairs where Yankee played his carpet riding games, static electricity picked up dog hair on each step completely coating the dress. The black, shimmering gown became a bristly white Harris Tweed, more suitable for a highland fling than a dinner party.

Yankee Doodle was with us for about four years when we noticed a growth on back of his neck. When the growth continued to increase, we brought him to Dr. O'Malley—considered an especially fine veterinarian. He operated on Yankee at his clinic in Clinton, Massachusetts, and then brought him to the Angell Memorial Hospital in Boston for cancer treatments. After a prolonged treatment period, a healthy dog came home to us. But soon after his return, disaster struck. He spied an attractive female Norwegian elkhound on the other side of the road and was hit by a car when he ran to make her acquaintance.

His hind legs were paralyzed. After medical attention, we arranged a large dog bed, well padded for Yankee's comfort. Here he lay, only able to prop himself up with his forelegs to eat or drink. Marianne was devastated by Yankee's condition but had a fortunate distraction. Two days after Yankee's accident, I rushed her to Hahneman Hospital where she gave birth to our son Eric on May 26, 1951. In those days, mothers and their newborns stayed in the hospital for close to a week. During that week, Yankee Doodle faded away. He died the day before Marianne and baby Eric came home. It was sad to lose a great dog, but upon reflection, we doubt that he would have accepted a newcomer into the household after receiving the full attention and affection of his mistress and master during his lifetime.

Oakholm was home to a series of memorable dogs. The first dog to come to the farm in 1925 was a large handsome German shepherd called Ned. He had originally been my grandmother's pet at Drury

Lane—given to her by Father shortly before she died. Father had attempted to train Ned, as Grandmother's crippling arthritis prevented her from doing so. The first lesson was to make sure the dog would come when called. Father's method was to tie a clothesline to his collar, call softly, and pull him steadily forward. Ned fought this procedure using all his eighty pounds of youthful muscle and with all four legs straining against the clothesline. After this, he would never let Father near him—even after Ned was brought to the farm.

Ned became a great farm dog. He was placed under the care of Stellan Peterson, our boss farmer, who taught him to patrol the buildings and watch over farm animals and assist in herding them. Although he had an amiable disposition, Ned was suspicious of strangers. With a low rumbling growl, he would keep visitors from exiting their cars until properly introduced. For twelve years he presided over all other animals at *Oakholm*, and until the day he died, would never let Father touch him—much to Father's extreme irritation.

On a summer afternoon in 1929, Father received a telephone call from Charles L. Allen, a founder and former chairman of the Norton Company, who owned acres of woods and a rustic house in Petersham. Father had worked for him for years and held him in high esteem. When Mr. Allen asked Father to visit, Father hopped into his Buick coupe with alacrity and drove the twenty-five miles to Allen's country house. When he returned about three hours later, we saw him reach into the back seat of the car and pick up something small, black, and fuzzy. It was a small Newfoundland puppy about three months old, a gift from Mr. Allen. Dick—for that was his name—grew and grew until he reached a weight of one hundred and fifty pounds. When he put his forepaws on your shoulder, he reached a height of six feet. He was magnificent—totally black with a heavy, glossy coat. Because of their thick, impenetrable fur, Newfoundlands are very uncomfortable in hot summer weather. To escape the heat, Dick waded into the waters of Lake Quaboag up to his armpits—not coming out until sunset with a matted, wet coat and an occasional lily pad draped around his neck.

One day Dick refused to come out of the water altogether. We dragged him out and found that he wasn't just affected by the heat. He was unable to stand and wouldn't eat. Finally after a trip to the vet, he coughed up an enormous ball of steel wool, which had been used to scour greasy pans. Thinking it especially tasty, Dick had swallowed it whole, and it had lodged somewhere between his throat and stomach.

In the cool of the fall, Dick enjoyed following the riding horses. One day our ride took us past Brookfield's most dilapidated farm—a place with unhealthy cattle and unhealthier looking people. A pack of mangy dogs also made their home there. We passed without incident, but eventually realized that Dick was no longer trotting behind. We thought he had gone home but upon our return, he was still missing in action. Retracing our route, we found him lying by the side of the road near the disreputable farm. He got up wagging his great tail and followed us back to the stable. We noticed that he limped slightly, and on closer inspection, saw that he had a cut near his nose and a bleeding scratch on his left ear. We eventually found out what had happened to him. Dick had been lured into the barn at Brookfield's worst farm, and a pack of dogs was locked in with him for sport. As it turned out, Dick killed three of the pack before the farmer could open the door to let him out. Though a good-natured animal, it was obvious that Dick could fight like a wild cat when cornered. Also his heavy fur protected him like a suit of armor.

We learned what had happened from the farmer himself, who wanted payment for the death of his three dogs. Father was enraged by this request—the farmer was lucky to get away with his life.

In their later years, Mother and Father had a succession of small dogs. They spent part of the year in Florida and found it easier to travel with small dogs rather than with the large varieties that one usually associates with a farm. Gammy, named after my Amherst fraternity, the Gamma Chapter of Psi Upsilon, was a Cairn terrier—small, wire-haired and light tan in color with pointed ears. He was devoted to my father. He lay next to him when he read the paper or when he was writing at his desk. Gammy followed him around the farm with occasional sorties to try to catch a squirrel or chipmunk. He rarely barked except when a stranger came or to greet Father when he had been away for a time. He was a brave little animal—sometimes foolishly so—as when he attempted to attack dogs twice his size.

Gammy was the only dog allowed in the dining room. He waited patiently under the table to receive any largesse. Father always thought he was covering up what he was doing, but a strange expression on his face and a certain tilt of his shoulders gave away the fact that he was feeding Gammy treats from his plate. Mother was always disgusted with this little secret game between Father and Gammy.

One of Gammy's adventures was almost his last. He had been missing for two days, and we searched the farm to no avail. In late afternoon on the second day, Ned, the German shepherd, tried to get the attention of his master, Stellan Peterson. He whined, took a few steps in a specific direction, and then whined again. Stellan realized that Ned was trying to lead him up the side of the hill near our two-thousand gallon water tank where the soil is gravelly. He heard the faint sound of barking which he traced to a woodchuck hole. Gammy was stuck. Stellan ran to our house to get a small shovel and tell us that our little dog had been found. Six of us gathered around the hole while Stellan carefully dug down to Gammy, expecting to find him near death. Freed by the last shovelful, he leapt out of his internment, shook the sand and gravel off his body, lifted his leg on a small white pine, and wagged his tail as if to say, "There was really nothing to worry about." Father, of course, was overjoyed and the following day bought two large bones for Ned as a reward for saving Gammy.

Our last dog at *Oakholm* was Rufus, a large white standard poodle weighing seventy-five pounds—a strong, beautiful, intelligent animal who lived with us for sixteen years. Since he didn't come to us until after our own children had left the nest, he was not used to small children. Therefore, when the grandchildren began to appear, Rufus became quite disturbed. They were getting the attention that he usually expected for himself. He was amazed and disgusted to see hairless animals moving around on their hands and knees and could not understand the odd noises they made. To him they also smelled bad. When the children and their parents came to the house, he did his best to avoid them—not always successfully. Cornered behind sofas or under beds by children squealing with delight, he growled in warning and nipped their outstretched hands. This brought howls from the children and angry reactions from their parents. One of these veterans of Rufus' ire, now a man of forty, still has a small scar on his neck which he shows with pride.

Rufus getting ready for an excursion in the farm truck (1980)

For Marianne and me, Rufus was a true friend. He sensed our moods. When we were happy, so was he—wagging his tail, making an occasional small bark, or raising a paw. If sadness prevailed, he would place his head on a lap or arm to show us, with his soulful eyes, that he understood our problem. The low growls, the whines, the barks, the expressions in his eyes, and the motions he made combined to form a language that was understandable to us. We were never lonely with him around. Rufus was also a fine watchdog, making it very clear to strangers that they were not to move towards doors or out of cars until approved by Marianne or me.

For a short time during his reign, Rufus had a companion, a black miniature poodle named Scruffy, about a third his size, weighing in at about twenty pounds. Rufus and Scruffy barely tolerated each other. When let out of the house in the morning, Scruffy would get into a minor fit if he wasn't first out the door. He insisted on being in the lead when they patrolled the farm. We see them in our minds' eyes trotting down our driveways and roads—the little black dog first, the big white dog behind—both with their tails straight up in the air.

A large weeping cherry tree marks the place where Rufus now lies. It is a beautiful specimen on a hillside at *Oakholm* surrounded by forest and meadow. Scruffy lies nearby under a blueberry bush.

A Wedding

In 2004, my daughter Ingrid decided to get married for the second time to Dany Pelletier. Her first wedding had been at *Oakholm* in 1978 and was an elegant affair orchestrated by her mother and me. This time around she and Dany wanted it their way. Shorts and T-shirts were the dress code and invitations went out by e-mail to the people that were important to them. The date was set for Saturday, July 5, 2003 to coincide with the family's traditional Fourth of July celebration.

The weather forecast was dicey. It called for hot, muggy air with a good chance of a thunderstorm in the afternoon. However, in addition to God, there were others working to make it a beautiful day. In the early morning, looking down the hill toward the lake and the lovely mirrored sunrise, we beheld a diaphanous figure engaged in a graceful dance, reaching out to several points of the compass with something in her hands. It was Ingrid's close friend, Jan Goddard-Taylor. She was clutching a quartz crystal—a symbol of good luck. Her performance was aimed at producing a fine wedding day, but more importantly, to bring good fortune to Ingrid and Dany.

Another harbinger of good luck that morning came when one of our great bald eagles dove to catch a fish very close to the tent where Ingrid and members of the family were setting up tables. The team consisted of Marianne, Ingrid, son John's wife, Giselle, and Jan, who decorated the round tables with pots of bright red impatiens, each planted with an American and Canadian flag representing the homelands of the bride and groom. Blue and red ribbons added elegance to each table. Fresh flowers adorned the buffet table. Despite some heated arguments over where to locate tables and things on them, the finished outcome was festive.

Long before the ceremony, one and a half hours early, Pastor Paul Kennedy and his wife Carol arrived. It fell upon myself to greet and entertain them as all the ladies were primping themselves for the wedding. I was still in sweaty working clothes and had many things left to do. But I was glad to stop everything to serve them iced tea and cookies in the library. With a wave of his hand, Paul spilled his large glass on a the rug, chair and himself, requiring rapid ministrations from his wife and host. Paul heads major charitable drives and carries on a multitude of pastoral and civic duties in Worcester.

I then ran down to the *J House* to berate the caterers who had not only come an hour early, but had driven over the grass to the tent and left large tracks. Back up the hill to the house I went to retrieve wine and other types of liquors. Meanwhile, Ingrid was issuing strident orders from the *J House*. I replied from a safe distance using a bull horn which did not seem to have a calming effect on her. The rest of the men folk set up additional tables and chairs outside the tent under the pines. Marcus McCorison efficiently took charge of the parking fields and meadows. During last-minute dressing, Ingrid was observed running away from Giselle who was chasing her with a curling iron.

At last it was one o'clock, the time guests were due to arrive. We stood ready to greet the wedding guests. But, for some time, no one but family came and we wondered what had happened. Had Dany and Ingrid done something awful that made them anathema to their friends? Had improper directions to *Oakholm* been sent with the internet invitations? Finally, a trickle of guests arrived followed by more and more, and we learned what had delayed them. Being Saturday, July fifth, most of the towns surrounding us were having Independence Day parades and had closed off their main streets without indicating detours. The guests' annoyance and dismay over delays of as much as an hour were soon swept away by the beauty of the day and the rapid consumption of liquid refreshments.

Nearing two o'clock, the scheduled time for the wedding ceremony, everyone was present at the *J House* lawn with two notable exceptions: Marie Harburger, who was to conduct the ceremony, and Dany, the groom, and his family. Ingrid was dismayed and visibly upset. But, the moment the clock struck two, we all looked up toward the flagpole and the house to see a small parade of Pelletiers coming down the hill. The bridegroom led the way, followed by his father and mother, and his sister and her family.

At the same time, Marie Harburger arrived in the parking area and hastily made her way to the spot where she was to conduct the ceremony. She motioned to Ingrid and Dany who came, hand in hand, before her. She began her homily, a testimony to the power of the marriage commitment. With the pronouncement came the exchange of rings. The rings were elegantly designed in gold and meteorite by Neal Rosenblum, a leading jeweler in Worcester—perhaps to bring them

Ingrid and Dany's wedding, Marie Harburger officiating (2004)

luck from outer space. Pastor Kennedy said a few appropriate words in his eloquent way. His theme was *Tov Me'od*, a Hebrew expression which he explained as "everything is as is it should be."

Ingrid insisted that we do our traditional Fourth of July production of the old Swedish drinking song, *Helan Går* (Bottoms Up), in which we sing a verse for each one ounce drink of *aquavit*. After each drink, we sing a chorus in stentorian tones, which can be heard by all who live on the shores of Lake Quaboag. For years, son Eric has poured the *aquavit* into the glasses, passed them around, and refilled them when empty. Although, he is very careful not to refill too many times, there are always a few who have insufficient stamina to handle the final round.

At the conclusion of the song, an unexpected event occurred. Ingrid's neighbor, Drew Goodwin, a distinguished figure topped by a good-looking, visored hat, came forward as Commodore of the Maynard Yacht Club and asked Marianne and myself to join him. He pronounced us honorary members of the club, and presented us with hats similar to his own. The Maynard Yacht Club has no yachts and its ocean is a small mill pond, but its members meet regularly at a local pub and are a mainstay in Maynard's annual parade.

We then repaired to the buffet table for sandwiches, salads, and a three-tiered wedding cake. On an outside corner of the tent stood a fine, wooden jardinière, made and given to the newlyweds by Josh Edgerly, Ingrid's cousin Vicki's husband. Guests were encouraged to fill it with cash to help finance the building of a deck at Ingrid and Dany's home in Maynard, but we noticed that most of them walked right by, pretending not to see it.

A significant moment of the afternoon came when a bevy of beauties gathered at the south wall of the *J House* to sing to the bride and groom who were seated before them on the golf cart. The song was entitled "Sisters" from the movie, *Holiday Inn*. Ingrid's sister, Muffy, and sister-in-law, Nancy, found the music and rehearsed and directed the singers. These included all the females in the clan, as well as a few of Ingrid's inner circle of friends.

As the great day wore on people began to leave and soon only dutiful family members were left to clean up. Ingrid and Dany had disappeared, having survived their wedding day with nothing left for them to do but contemplate a life of wedded bliss. Marianne and I collapsed on our porch, martinis in hand, to relive the days events.

Silos

THERE ARE TWO STRUCTURES at *Oakholm* that are admired more than any other—the silos. Artists have painted them, and many people have photographed them. The silos were built to store chopped corn for cows to eat during the fall, winter, and early spring—seasons when green grass in the pastures is either killed by frost or covered with snow.

The silos are round, and are twenty-eight feet high and nearly eight feet in diameter. They are covered by twelve-sided, double-angled, dark grey slate roofs which add six feet to their overall height. A copper weather vane of "The Cow that Jumped Over the Moon" tops the higher of the two silos. Although both silos are exactly the same height, one is higher because it was built on higher ground. The siding of each is curved ceramic tile measuring a foot square. The outer sides of the tiles are glazed with colors ranging from dark-reddish brown to light tan. A small dormer with a white window provides an opening in each silo for the pipe used to blow the chopped corn into the storage chamber.

There used to be a large electric motor near the silos which powered a contraption with several industrial knives attached to its center. Corn stalks driven by a conveyer were fed into the knives which whirled around at a high speed. The knives had a double function. They not only

The silos at Oakholm, *detail (2007)*
Painted by Bruce Davidson

cut the corn stalks into small pieces, but also blew the pieces into a pipe which ran up the outside of the silo and into the dormer window. The corn fed our Guernsey cows for months.

There was still a lot of hand and horse labor involved in harvesting cattle corn when we first came to *Oakholm* in the 1920s. The corn field was prepared like a hay field—plowed, fertilized, and harrowed. A horse-drawn seed planter placed the seeded rows at three-foot intervals. Seeding was always done across the down slopes of hilly fields to prevent soil erosion. Until the corn was about four feet high, it was kept weed-free by a man steering a one-horse cultivator—something like a small plow. When the corn had reached a height of four feet, it was strong enough to grow well without further cultivating.

We harvested the corn in late summer, usually in early September. This allowed the stalks to fully mature and the ears to reach full size. Good cattle corn grew as high as eight to ten feet—"high as an elephant's eye"—which is much higher than sweet corn. Corn was cut at the base of the stalks by men wielding knives attached at right angles to wooden handles. The blades had a sharp, wavy cutting edge. It was hard physical work, requiring a bent-over position and a strong arm to cut through the corn stalks. The stalks were thrown onto a horse-drawn wagon which Molly and Bess, our two Percherons, pulled to the silos. There, they were thrown on a conveyor belt which fed them into the whirling knives.

Covered by a building connected to the cow barn, a steel ladder built into the wall of each silo allowed men to reach the level of the corn silage. There they pitched the silage down onto a wheeled cart. The filled cart was then pushed to the mangers in the cow barn where the cows ate it with gusto. As time elapsed, the silage fermented slightly, which made it even more appealing to our happy cows.

I was not able to handle the task of corn harvesting until I was in my teens. I simply did not have the strength to cut the stalks and throw them on and off the wagons. However, there was one job that appealed to me, and that I could do at the age of ten. When the small pieces of corn were blown into the silo, they formed a cone-shaped pile. From time to time, this had to be leveled out so that the corn packed evenly and filled the silo to its maximum capacity. With a short handled rake, I climbed the interior ladder to the right level, jumped into the silo and leveled out the corn. It was always cool in there. The silage had a fresh, sweet smell, and my imagination ran wild. I became a variety of heroes. The silo became a castle tower and I the was great knight defending it. Or I became a prisoner like the Count of Monte Christo, who was desperately searching for a means of escape. My daydreams were usually ended by a shower of silage, signifying that a new load of corn was being processed.

The silos are now empty. There are no cows to feed. Even if there were cows, they would be fed their corn silage in a different way. These days silage is usually piled in pastures under heavy plastic sheets that are pulled back gradually to allow cattle to eat their daily allotments outside, a much cheaper and simpler method. There is no need for expensive silos, and there is much less labor. So, what do we do with these silos—these handsome, ceramic structures which everyone loves to look at?

In many ways, these magnificent structures have come to represent *Oakholm*. No longer used for their original purpose, they nevertheless are lovingly maintained because they are beautiful. *Oakholm* has evolved over the years from an active dairy and horse farm to one that produces crops from forest and field. But perhaps its most important function is as a beacon and meeting place for family.

Nothing is as important as the maintenance of a strong family, a family whose members love and respect each other and help each other. When we arrived at *Oakholm* in 1925 we were five. Now, four generations and eighty-two years later, we are forty, ranging in age from six to ninety. All have left their mark on *Oakholm* and *Oakholm* is a part of who they are. It is the place the family comes together.

About the Cover Illustrations

THESE MURALS decorating the play room at *Oakholm* were painted by Arthur Sinclair Covey (1877-1960). The originals are each approximately eight-feet long by two-feet high and form a colorful frieze around the room depicting events in the life of the farm.

Arthur Covey became a well known muralist and painted extensive designs at the headquarters of the Kohler Company in Wisconsin. He also painted the panels on the ceiling of the Knave of the Trinity Lutheran Church in Worcester, Massachusetts. In 1921, he married the Newberry Award winning children's book illustrator, Lois Lenski. Arthur and Lois were close friends of George N. Jeppson and his wife, Selma. They visited *Oakholm* many times.

Acknowledgments

MANY INDIVIDUALS assisted me in the preparation of this book. Collectively, they are TidePool Press, a talented and hard-working group of editors, designers and photographers. Their help and advice in knitting together a group of stories and memories from past and present into a cohesive book have been invaluable.

This book would have been impossible without the consistent encouragement of my wife, Marianne. She has provided my first tier of editing not to mention hours of reluctant typing and e-mailing. My gratitude comes, as always, with my love.